Breeding Tomatoes for Processing: History and Potential

ATPBR
Breeding for Prosperity

ADVANCED TRAINING IN PLANT BREEDING (ATPBR)

A15, Amrut Sai Sara City, Nakshtrawadi, Paithan Road, Aurangabad, Maharashtra-431001

nipa®

NIPA® GENX ELECTRONIC RESOURCES & SOLUTIONS P. LTD.

New Delhi-110 034

Dr. Aparna Tiwari
Co-Founder, Director – ATPBR

Aparna Tiwari is Co-founder and Chief Executive Officer at the Foundation for Advanced Training in Plant breeding (ATPBR), where she leads professional training, technology liaising, awareness sessions, and other capacity building activities. She has worked previously in various positions with the FAO (Food and Agriculture Organization), Monsanto India Pvt. Ltd., ICRISAT (International Crops Research Institute for the Semi-Arid Tropics), and the MGM– Institute of Technology. She obtained her MSc and PhD from the Wageningen University, The Netherlands, and her Bachelor's (BSc) from Banaras Hindu University sity. She has authored two books and published several research papers in peer-reviewed international journals and conferences.

About ATPBR

ATPBR is a registered not-for-profit Foundation, based in India, which works in close collaboration with Seed Industry, Institutions, NGOs, and Government bodies, to impart training in plant breeding to develop future-ready plant breeders. It is India's leading networking training organization, with full-fledged expertise and resources for capacity building, market linkages, policy advocacy, and project management. Main objective of ATPBR is to develop a sustainable and thriving agricultural system to serve farmers, support emerging entrepreneurs and assist industries to build market-driven competencies in Human Resources. ATPBR is open to collaborate with diverse range of organizations, academic and research institutions, NGOs, independent professionals and aspire to meet the intellectual needs to make crop improvement an attractive and lucrative domain for all concerned.

Dr. Surinder K Tikoo
Co-Founder and Research Advisor
Tierra AgriTech Ltd., Pune

Speaker

Dr Surinder K Tikoo, currently Co-Founder and Research Advisor, Tierra AgriTech Ltd., Pune, has five decades of experience as a successful vegetable breeder, teacher, and research & development manager. He has held global leadership positions over long periods in two private sector organizations, as well as spent 20 years with the Indian Council of Agricultural Research (ICAR) as a vegetables breeder, teacher, and research guide. He has developed several nationally and internationally released varieties and hybrids of tomato and okra, some of which are market leaders in their respective segments. He has served on several advisory committees of the Government of India and various professional bodies. Dr Tikoo, a PhD from Bangalore University, has published over 50 research and review papers. He also holds one patent. He has been conferred the Life Time Achievement Award for Excellence in Translational Research, jointly by the Society of Plant Biochemistry & Biotechnology and Springer.

Dr. Sharan Angadi
Director, ATPBR, and
Former Head of Research
Asia Pacific Region, Nunhems Seeds

Moderator

Dr Sharan Angadi is a plant geneticist and breeder who worked for 17 years in India, first with UAS, Bangalore, and then with the Indian Council for Agricultural Research (ICAR), contributing significantly to the genetic improvement of oilseed crops and horticultural crops. He then devoted 22 years to Pro Agro PGS and Nunhems Seeds, Netherlands, where he served as Head of Breeding for Asia Pacific and Global Coordinator for peppers, spanning several countries in Asia, Europe, and the Americas. He has particular experience in applying emerging technologies to viable commercial plant breeding. Dr Angadi has a PhD from IARI, New Delhi; an MSc from Tamil Nadu Agricultural University, Coimbatore; and a BSc from UAS, Bangalore. After retirement, he continues to provide expert R&D advice to seed companies in India and abroad, besides serving on various expert bodies. The Asia & Pacific Seed Association (APSA) has honoured him with The Most Influential Plant Breeding Researcher for Horticultural Crops award for the year 2021.

Breeding Tomatoes for Processing: History and Potential

WebCon Series 22

Dr. Surinder K Tikoo
Co-Founder & Research Advisor
Tierra Agrotech Ltd
Hyderabad

ATPBR
Breeding for Prosperity

ADVANCED TRAINING IN PLANT BREEDING (ATPBR)
A15, Amrut Sai Sara City, Nakshtrawadi, Paithan Road, Aurangabad, Maharashtra-431001

NIPA® GENX ELECTRONIC RESOURCES & SOLUTIONS P. LTD.
New Delhi-110 034

ADVANCED TRAINING IN PLANT BREEDING (ATPBR)

NIPA® GENX ELECTRONIC
RESOURCES & SOLUTIONS P. LTD.

101,103, Vikas Surya Plaza, CU Block
L.S.C.Market, Pitam Pura, New Delhi-110 034
Ph : +91 11 27341616, 27341717, 27341718
E-mail: newindiapublishingagency@gmail.com
Website: www. nipabooks.com

For customer assistance, please contact
Phone: + 91-11-27 34 17 17
Fax: + 91-11-27 34 16 16
E-Mail: feedbacks@nipabooks.com

ISBN: 978-93-58871-41-8

Published and Exclusively Distributed by NIPA

"This WebCon is compiled and transcribed by Dr. M.J. Vasudeva Rao, currently a member of the Training Advisory Board of ATPBR"

Edited by Aruna T. Kumar

Composed and Designed by NIPA®.

Preface

ATPBR is bringing eminent plant breeders who have achieved laurels in not just science of plant breeding, but have excelled in other related areas like policy, administration, etc., to meet practicing and potential plant breeders on a platform called ATPBR Webinar series regularly every month. These Web-based Conferences (WebCon) have been hugely successful as seen by the numbers of participants from India and outside of India. The WebCon series captures the presentations in a published format which includes key messages delivered by the speakers.

Contents

Breeding Tomatoes for Processing History and Potential

Surinder K Tikoo

A few months back when Sharad Deshpande was talking about some processing tomatoes, I said that there is a lot of history behind processing tomatoes. He said then why don't you speak on the subject and I said why not. So that is how this talk happened. First, I thought I will speak on breeding tomatoes as its history is even more interesting than what has happened later. I had heard a story when I went to USA for the first time in 1982. I was with Dr Charlie Rick, the father of tomato genetics, in his lab in USDA, UC, Davis, California. He talked about how the processing industry happened, who bred the types suitable for processing, how 80 percent of processing tomatoes of the USA came from California, where we are today and what could be done in this area.

Why is Tomato Nutritionally Important

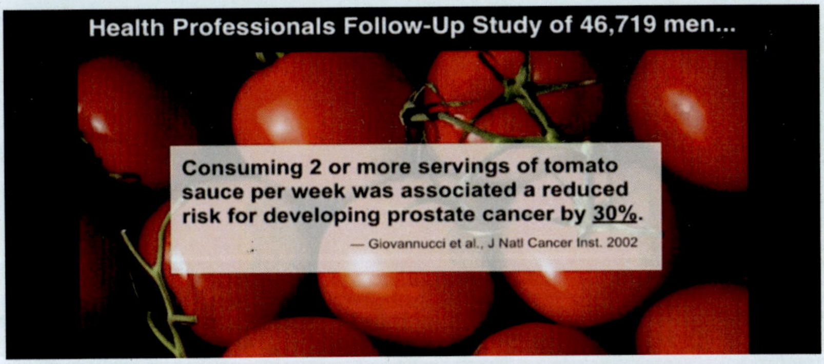

Medical science is focussing on metabolomes as future of patient treatment

Before we get into the main topic, let us take a quick look at tomato as a nutritionally important crop. One of the scientists at National Cancer Institute has said that consuming two or more servings of tomato sauce per week is associated with a 30 per cent reduced risk of developing prostate cancer as tomatoes have lycopene in tomatoes which is an antioxidant and has anti-cancerous properties. It also has vitamin C and the juice is acidic. Medical science is now focusing on metabolomes as a future of means of treatment for diseases. What is happening today in the U.S and some other advanced countries is that they have discovered that everybody has a different gut metabolome and therefore, the line of treatment needs to be personalized for each human being. Hence any new patient going to a doctor will have his/her metabolome studied and use bioinformatics to study which medicine helped someone with a similar metabolome & prescribe the same medicine. Tomatoes of future with the enhanced nutrient contents can become like eating a nutritious capsule to be given to the patients.

UMAMI – Flavour – A key to why Tomato is addictive

- Generally, umami taste is common to foods that contain high levels of L-glutamate,
- IMP (Inosinic acid)
- GMP (Guanosine monophosphate)

Most notably in fish, shellfish, cured meats, meat extracts, mushrooms, vegetables (e.g., ripe tomatoes, Chinese cabbage, spinach, celery, etc.), green tea, hydrolyzed vegetable protein, and fermented and aged products involving bacterial or yeast cultures, such as cheeses, shrimp pastes, fish sauce, soy sauce, nutritional yeast, and yeast extracts such as Vegemite and Marmite.[3][39]

And the other thing is to understand why we get addicted to tomato. This is due to its umami taste which is common to foods that contain high levels of alpha glutamate. These chemicals give the particular flavour to tomato fruits. Similarly, Chinese cabbage, spinach, and other vegetables have their own special flavours. Tomato can thus become addictive and the more we breed for its flavour and other qualities, their addiction can make people like tomatoes even more.

Scope

- Context
- Few definitions
- Processing Tomatoes – Where it began & Lessons
- Global scenario of processing tomatoes today
- Agronomy – key factors
- Breeding of Varieties/Hybrids
    - Critical Traits bred over time – in India
- Possible scenario to increase processing production

This is the structure of my talk today and their context. I will cover a few definitions, a brief history of where the processing tomatoes began, the lessons we have learnt, the global scenario, key factors of agronomy that help in making the production of better processing tomatoes, breeding of varieties and hybrids over time, and possible scenarios to increase processing tomato production especially with reference to India. On the right is a picture of mechanically-harvested tomatoes in California.

Context

- **Global Tomato importance as a crop**
- **No Tomato no cooking but 99% Fresh tomatoes used**
- **20 mmt of tomato from 810K ha @ 25 t/ha productivity & only 150,000 tonnes processed.**
- **Just 1% processed – while USA, Italy, China process over 70 % & export to the world earning billions of dollars.**
- **India imported canned tomato, sauce and paste worth 20.64 $M 2019, a 146 % over 2018 .**
- **Nearly 72% of the imports were from China followed by USA, Spain, Italy and Chile.**
- **Because of not having enough processing we lose 40 to 50 percent of the produce in the glut season (rabi)**
- **Because farm gate prices fall to a level when farmers don't cover even the harvesting costs.**
- **Current varieties/hybrids not specifically bred for processing quality –**
    - **TSS/Brix/Acidity, Viscoscity, Colour & Transportability, Concentrated maturity**
- National Academy of Agricultural Sciences (NAAS) organized a Brain Storming Session (BSS)**on "Need for Breeding Tomatoes Suitable for Processing" on November 24, 2020 with Dr. A.T. Sadashiva (Convener) under the Co-Chairmanship of Dr. D.P. Ray, Former Vice-Chancellor, OU&AT.**
- **The BSS was attended by eminent scientists, experts and processors from India and abroad in the relevant disciplines.**

The global importance of tomato as a crop is as much because of processing into various products as it is for the fresh market. Processing has not yet taken root in India although a total of 20 million metric tonnes of tomato are grown from 810,000 hectares in India. Our average productivity is 25 tonnes per hectare which is very low. Of the 20 million metric tonnes produced in India, only 150,000 tonnes are processed, which is just about one percent of our total production. However, in other countries like the USA and China, they process nearly 70 percent of their tomato production. This has been the case for the last many years and has not really increased although lately many companies are getting interested in processing tomatoes. India imported canned tomato and sauce worth 20.6 million dollars in 2019 which was a 146 percent increase over 2018. Nearly 72 percent of the imports were from China followed by the US, Spain, Italy and Chile. Because of not doing enough processing, we lose 40 to 50 percent of the produce when there is a seasonal glut in production, especially in the rabi season. Many of you must have known that especially during the February to April period, we know that Kolar farmers throw tomato fruits on the road because they don't get the right price. At such times, the farm gate prices crash to a level that even the harvesting costs cannot be recovered leading to the farmers not even harvesting the crop. Current tomato varieties in India are not specifically bred for processing quality traits. Though many of them have one or the other traits, specifically we don't breed for processing types in India as the processing industry has not developed well. Because of all these reasons, it was on 24 November 2020, Dr A.T. Sadashiva, Ex Head of Vegetable Crops, ICAR-IIHR, Bangalore, under the chairmanship of Dr D P Ray, former Vice Chancellor of Odisha University of Agriculture & Technology, organized a brainstorming session under the auspices of NAAS, National Academy of Agricultural Sciences, on the topic "Need for Breeding Tomatoes Suitable for Processing". Many of us were involved in presenting papers in the brain storming session to develop strategies to help develop this type of tomato. The papers presented during the meeting are available from NAAS. I will be referring to some of those papers here. Thanks to Dr Sadashiva for having shared them with me.

Few Definitions

- **Ketchup is made with tomatoes, sugar, vinegar/acetic acid and spices.** Also, ketchup is cold in nature and is never served hot
- **Sauce is made from tomatoes, oil, meat or vegetable stock, spices and never uses vinegar**. All varieties of sauces are served hot.
- **Juice isn't cooked & it's more watery than sauce**
- **Purée** is a blended mixture of**cooked and strained tomatoes** created by mixing ripe tomatoes, salt & citric acid (like lemon juice) using a blender or food processor.
- **Paste** is a thick paste made by cookingtomatoesfor several hours to reduce the water content, straining out the seeds and skins, and cooking the liquid again to reduce the base to a thick, rich concentrate

Before getting into the core topic, I would like to define a few more terms in the area of processed tomatoes for some of you who may not be familiar with them. Ketchup is made with tomato, sugar, vinegar or acetic acid and spices. Ketchup is cold and it is never served hot. Sauce is made from tomatoes, oil, meat or vegetable stock and spices, and does not use vinegar. All varieties of sauces are served hot. One can buy these sauces off the shelf and also one can make them at home. They need to be served hot or one can mix vegetables or meat into the sauce and cook them so it has a tangy taste. Juice is not cooked and it is waterier than sauce. Juice, these days, is extracted through cold pressing so that the lycopene, other vitamins and nutrients are not degraded during the extraction process. For making juice, one would need a different kind of tomato variety which has more juice than the normal tomato varieties. Puree is a blend of cooked and strained tomatoes created by mixing ripe tomatoes, salt, citric acid and lemon juice, and other ingredients for preservation. Tomato paste is a thick paste made by cooking tomatoes for several hours to reduce the water content.

China took away almost 20 percent of California's share in the global processed tomatoes market and this was possible because their government supported the farmers with ground level help to create the right infrastructure. They now make paste for export which is also imported into India. This paste is made by dehydrating tomatoes to a level that they can be transported in large boxes and plastic bags which can be shipped around the world.

Gordie C. Hanna

(July 1, 1903 – December 23, 1993)

- Known as "Jack" Hanna) was a University of California-Davis agronomy professor who helped revolutionize the tomato-growing industry. He won the John Scott Award in 1976 for his development of a **tomato variety capable of being machine-harvested**.[1] The variety **VF 145** came to be known as the "square tomato," being slightly blockier, preventing it from rolling off conveyor belts.[2]
- His concept was met with little support, in terms of both its technical feasibility and its anticipated negative impact on California agricultural labor."[3]
- **Genes sp, easy removal (later j/j2 genes), CFM**
- **Labour was becoming expensive**
- **The existing harvester was not suitable**
- **Joined with Engineer Coby Lorenzen to develop first harvester with Ernest Blackwelder – by 1963 first machines were working**

Source – Above & as told to SKTikoo by Prof Charlie Rick in 1982

I would now like to briefly talk about breeding of processing tomatoes. I think no talk on breeding of processing tomatoes can be done without referring to Dr. Gordie Hanna, more popularly known as Jack Hanna. He was a Professor at University of California and was a tomato breeder. He won the 'John Scot Award' in 1976 for development of machine-harvestable tomato varieties, which revolutionized mechanical handling of tomatoes. It was called VF145 and came to be known as the first square tomato though it was not really square in shape. It had a slightly oblong shape with one side pointed. Because of this shape, it was blockier and was not rolling off the conveyor belts during harvest. I will explain that when we go into mechanical harvesting. In one of his interviews with one Dickman, he said that he first thought of machine-harvestable tomatoes in 1942 and finally he got to start working on it in the late 1950s. Then, he talked about it with people in the University of California, Davis and also with people in the canning industry. He asked why can't we breed a tomato that can be harvested by a machine and they used to laugh at this thought. They thought that he was mad. He did not listen to them and he started talking to an agricultural engineer named Corey, at UC, Davis. They started talking about what was needed. For easy harvesting, they needed a plant type that has no vine so that it doesn't need staking and will grow on the ground, and have more fruits maturing together. During those times, labour was becoming expensive in California and the government was thinking to stop labour coming from Mexico to California. That was also causing problems to the canners because the relatively less-expensive Mexican labour was being used for harvesting. They were paid on a daily basis and were relatively cheaper. The existing harvesters that were already developed for asparagus and other vegetables were not suitable for tomatoes. So Jack Hanna joined engineer

Coby Lorenzen to develop the first harvester with the help of Blackwelder Manufacturing Company. Blackwelder used to make tractors and he was one among the first in 1963 to build workable machines for tomato harvesting. This led to a harvesting machinery industry that, in the USA alone, is about three billion US dollars' worth used for Tomato harvesting for processing purposes.

Jack Hannah - Contd

- Hanna had a simple test for his tomatoes: He would throw them onto the road by the experimental farm at UC Davis, and breed the ones that survived.
- It took nearly 20 years between breeding road-resistant tomatoes and building the machines that would pick them before Hanna and his engineer colleague, Coby Lorenzen, got it right with the VF-145 tomato (called the "square tomato" because it wouldn't roll) and the Blackwelder mechanical tomato harvester.
- But this invention didn't take place in a vacuum. Hanna and Lorenzen were working against time. National opinion had turned against the dreaded Mexican, leading to things like the Eisenhower administration's subtly named Operation Wetback. The bracero program was going to be phased out, leaving California's processed tomato industry with no one exploit. Kick out the Mexicans, and what happens to the ketchup? The square tomato and the mechanical tomato harvester saved the processed tomato industry. In five years, over 95 percent of processing tomatoes in California were picked by machine.
- There was one problem, though: The square tomatoes sucked.
- **America's Tomatoes Taste Like Garbage (Because Of Racism)**

There is an interesting interview with Jack Hanna, his wife and also Charlie Rick at UC Davis library. A couple of things that one learns from that interview is that his wife said that she used to be a "breakfast widow" because Jack used to leave home at three o'clock in the morning to drive to the field for his work. One day a person came to meet her in the morning and asked, where is Jack? She said he is working and he looked at her very inquisitively. She said that she has no regrets because of the honours that Jack got later on. This teaches us dedication to one's work. Charlie Rick said that Jack used to discuss with him (Charlie) about his projects and Charlie gave him a lot of wild germplasm. The jointless gene came from one of those germplasm lines. I think he gave it to one of his students and the quantity was only 4–5 grams of seeds, but it had the jointless gene. Jointless gene means the tomato fruit comes off at the end of the pedicel so it is easier to harvest. But it has to be firm enough not to fall off while the plants are being harvested. So, they found the right gene and other pleiotropic effects associated with it which is the J2 gene of today. Jack used to harvest tomato fruits with his hands and throw them to the ground. He would then select plants whose fruits did not break in one or two throws and advance it to the next generation for further selection. It took him almost five or six years before he was able to derive lines from crosses that he made from collections like Red Top he received from a professor from New York.

Some VF (*Verticillium* & *Fusarium* wilts) resistant materials were developed in this process and from that emerged a variety called VF 145. He used pure line breeding and pedigree selection to develop these lines. He selected each and every line by using the throwing method to select for relative firmness. These lines were machine-harvestable. It took approximately seven to eight years to come out with the first prototype of the machine for harvesting these genotypes. This development coincided with Eisenhower's policy of stopping Mexican labour. For the canning industry it was a boom that by then the tomato breeders had developed such tomatoes. However, there was one problem - just that people thought that these tomatoes did not have good taste as they were having more alcohol-soluble solids, and less soluble salts. This is true to a large extent even today. I was lucky to get a chance to observe such tomatoes in 1982 in the fields at California as an UNDP fellow. They used to do direct seeding and used to plant hundreds of hectares in quick time using tractors with seed dibblers. The seeds were coated to make the dibbling easy and also provide seeds with some protection from diseases.

Key Lessons for Breeders from Jack Hannah Story

- Dedication
- Observational powers
- Genes don't show themselves unless one plants in right place & looks hard
- IPS works if you have the eyes – VF 36
- Convinced you can create a market where none existed - **PERSIST**

We can understand from Jack Hanna's work that dedication and observational powers are very important for breeders. Genes don't show themselves up unless one plants in the right place and looks hard. I think this is the basis for the genesis of what we call product development activities today. if we don't do testing of the hybrids in hot spots, or test the segregating materials in hot spots, it is not possible to select the right material. I did this in Pioneer, I did this in Syngenta, I did this in Advanta and I continue to do the same because without that even if the gene may be there we will not be able to recognize it. Unless we go to a hot spot for testing, the genes do not express. Also, markers are not available for every gene, so we need to have breeders with good eyes so that individual plant selection can successfully be implemented. There is a story about the development of VF36. VF36 was one of the first varieties for the fresh market that Jack Hanna developed. He was able to grow it in different places and a need to develop heat tolerance in these tomatoes emerged. This trait was needed because some of the farmers wanted to plant a little late which would experience the heat during the season. So, he kept on observing individual plant selections from this variety and developed what was called VF36 from which line came the earliest heat tolerant varieties. Lastly, if we are convinced, then we can create a market where none existed. Jack Hanna tried to convince the processors, the professors at UCD and the university funders. But they did not get convinced. So, he and Corey developed it on their own with whatever little funds they had. He said in an interview that he used to grow four or five rows extra and earn from those extra rows as a fresh market produce and used the proceeds to fund the research. He said that the cost for developing this was about forty-two thousand dollars but when they said that to the administrators, they laughed at them. By the time they were convinced that this is a great innovation, they said that the actual cost was $ 350,000 by including all the administrative costs.

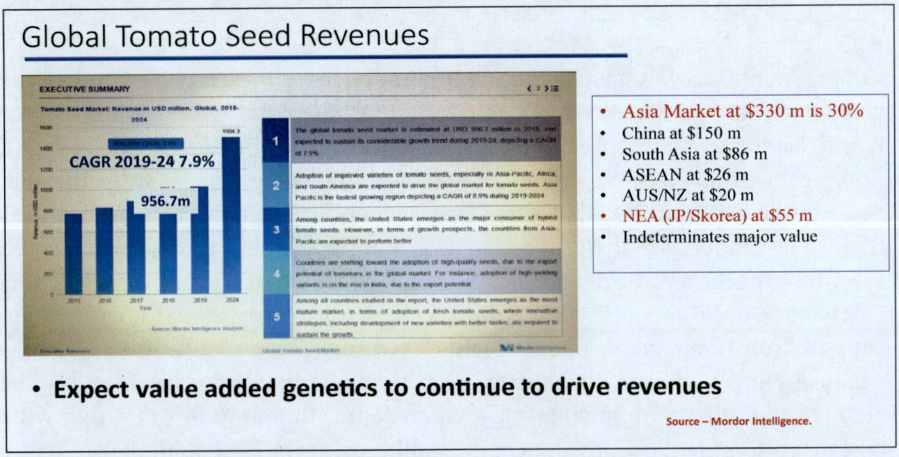

Now let us look at the global tomato seed revenue. I think we all know that the estimated total tomato seed market is 1.5 billion USD by 2024 as per Mordor Intelligence. The Asian market is a 330-million-dollar market which is 30 percent of the global market. Information about China, South Asian countries, and other Asian country markets are all in the slide. It is the indeterminates which have the highest value. In Europe, the indeterminate hybrids seeds for polyhouses cultivation are sold at about ten thousand dollars a kilo. For open field cultivation, they are sold between four thousand to six thousand dollars a kilo in developed countries. And, in India we are selling the same at about 500 dollars a kilo. This shows that there is an opportunity for indeterminates in the Indian market – high quality & high yield potential of three to four times the open field yields can help lower the pressure on land. In addition, the value-added genetics of nutritional quality and better taste will continue to drive these revenues.

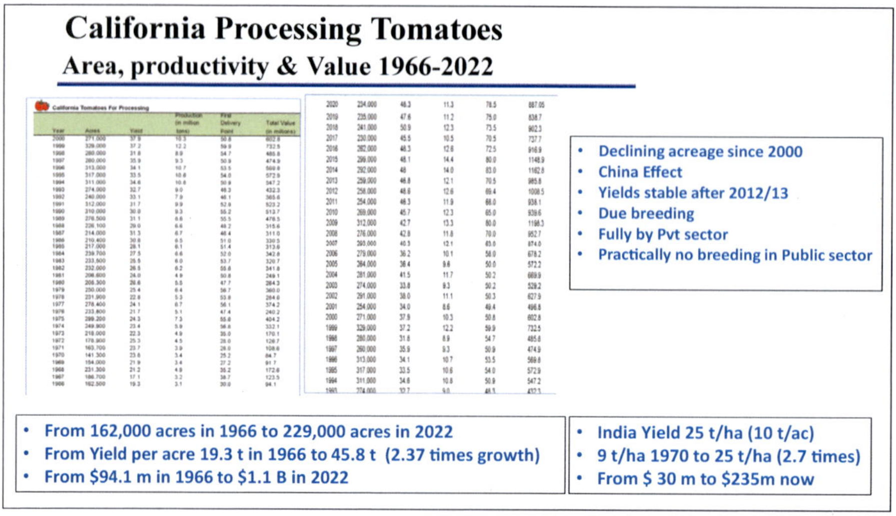

Let me mention a few facts about California because they are the number one processing state of the number one processing-tomato producing country in the world. Eighty five percent of processed tomatoes are produced in California and 30 percent of the world's processed tomatoes also originate from California. So, one can see from this data that there is a decline since 2000 because China took away 20 percent of world production and the Chinese government helped the Chinese farmers to develo[p the processing industry in northwest China where it is cold and dry. Now China is a major exporter of tomatoes with support from their government. Yields have now been stable since 2012-13 because there is not much happening in terms of increasing the yields. The area has not increased much as of now. The contribution to this is fully by the private sector. From 38 breeders in the public sector in 1982 in the USA, today only 4 or 5 breeders are left in the public sector. Bulk of the breeding work is done by the private sector, and practically there are no hybrids or varietal breeding in the public sector except in one place, i.e., Ashville, North Carolina. At other places, only trait breeding is carried out. From 162,000 acres in 1966, it went to 229,000 acres and the yield went up from 19.3 tonnes to 45.8 tonnes, which is a 2.37 times growth in total production. In value terms, it went up from about 95 m USD to 1.1 billion USD. In India, in the same period, yields went up from about 10 tonnes per hectare to 25 tonnes per hectare. In value terms, it went up from 30 million USD to 235 million USD. California is producing 1.1 billion USD worth of processing tomatoes currently. So, there is a gap that we need to fill.

Few Key Traits of Processing Tomatoes in USA

What are the differences between storebought tomatoes and processed tomatoes?

- **1. processed tomatoes are harvested ripe and red 2. processed tomatoes are used immediately, from the moment of harvesting less than 6 hours pass** until the tomato is in the car**3. processing tomatoes are completely machine harvested**

How do tomatoes survive transport?

- These tomatoes have been selectively bred for over 50 years to be quite different from the tomato you would buy. One of the qualities they have is **much thicker skin than fresh tomatoes, it is this property that allows them to survive the weight of 25,000 to 50,000 pounds of tomatoes without suffering much damage.**

How much does a tomato truck hold?

- A typical tomato truck holds **50,000 pounds of tomatoes, which is about 300,000 tomatoes.**

Why are tomato trucks uncovered?

- Time. During the height of the season, California tomato growers are producing 2,000,000,000 pounds tomatoes per week! To put that in perspective that is **40,000 tomato trucks each carrying 300,000 tomatoes Too much labour & costs.** The other main reason is that since tomato harvest is in the summer **covering the trucks could result in the tomatoes being damaged by the trapped heat.**

Interesting Quotes

- **Every rule has an exception, and tomatoes are clear that when it comes to the old saying, "If it tastes good, it must be bad for you." Recent scientific studies have discovered that tomatoes are not only delicious and versatile but loaded with health benefits.**
- **GET CANNED, GET HEALTHY** The Lycopene in cooked and processed tomatoes (sauce, paste, salsa, canned tomatoes) is more **easily absorbed than in raw tomatoes.** Conclusion: let the ketchup flow!
- To view the complete Tomatoes & Health Report in Adobe PDF format.

Let us talk about a few traits of processing tomatoes in the USA. Processing tomatoes are harvested ripe and red so that they are transported from the fields within six hours or so after harvest to the processing centres. For this, the tomatoes need enough firmness to be reaching the processing factory in six hours without getting squished or cracking open, and they also need enough firmness because each bin is loaded with 50000 pounds of tomatoes. For such a load, tomatoes need to be very firm so that they can sustain distance transportation. This trait has been used by breeders for our fresh market tomatoes in India in the last three decades or so very effectively. Since 2000, we have some very firm tomatoes, both in oval and square round types, which are not typical fresh market tomatoes and also can be used for processing. They also have much thicker skin than fresh market tomatoes. A typical tomato truck holds 50,000 pounds of tomato which is around 300,000 tomatoes. These trucks are not covered while the tomatoes are transported from farmer's fields to the processing centres, because it would be too costly to cover 40,000 tomato trucks, as it means too much labour, and other costs. Then it would also create heat which would damage the tomatoes. Interestingly, it was commonly said that if tomatoes are eaten in larger quantities they can be bad for one's health. But scientific studies have now clearly demonstrated that tomatoes are not only delicious and versatile, but also are loaded with health benefits. So, they are canned and hence last longer. Lycopene, the main element of health in tomatoes, is better absorbed when it is cooked. For more details on the nutritional quality of tomatoes, please refer to the website www.healthifyme.com.

Now I would like to show a short video on how tomatoes are harvested mechanically (Jack Hanna's breeding work led to many useful traits which made such harvest of processing tomatoes possible) *https://youtu.be/PqrOAVt75gc?si=WkjwCj5g3K3YLgAk*. In this video, we can see that the tractor is removing tomatoes from the ground and then it goes on to a conveyor belt where they are shaken and the jointless gene helps them to break the tomatoes free and the tomatoes are dropped into a bin below. The empty vines then fall back on the ground. They are empty vines because of the jointless gene. This is how the processing tomatoes are harvested and this is a quick view of how it happens.

Agronomy – key success factors USA etc

- Direct seeded to transplants today – Hybrids as key factor
  - From 100,000 plants /ha to around 40,000 today
- Professional seedling transplant growers
- Mulching & Drip Irrigation to save operational costs
- Seed coatings
- Close monitoring by farmers & extension advisors – CTGA in Ca
- Ethrel for once over harvests
- Deep Ploughing – 25% increase (reaching genetic potential)

Let us look at which agronomic and breeding traits contributed to the success of processing tomatoes in California. I will talk about the traits later, but the agronomic aspects first. The farmers have moved completely from direct seeded to transplanted tomatoes today. Of course, today, it is also because hybrids have overtaken the OP varieties. It becomes very expensive to do direct seeding of hybrid seeds as in direct seeded crop the population required is three or four times more & hence would be uneconomical. They have successfully moved to transplanting and with that the professional seedling-for-transplantation growers (nursery men) have become business entities that have developed over the years. Mulching and drip irrigation are used to save on operational costs. Seed coating is an essential part of better agronomy. All seeds are coated so that they germinate uniformly and are protected from fungal infections till they are transplanted. While farmers closely monitor their crops, they also have extension advisors. That is why they set up the California Tomato Growers Association (CTGA) in the 40s. The Association helps the processing of tomatoes immensely. I will talk about it later. During months of July to September, once-over harvesters are used by all. When around 30 percent of the fruits are ripe and the rest are in different ripening stages, they use ethrel 250 ppm to 500 ppm spray and 15 days later the machines harvest these tomatoes all at once. An agronomic experiment that was carried out was on studying the response of deep ploughing, which helps in deeper penetration of the roots, on yield. They had reported a 25 per cent increase in yields in the same varieties with deep ploughing. These practices ensure that the genetic potential for yield in these hybrids is fully harnessed

California Tomato Growers Assoc – CTGA

Key success factor for Ca Processing Tomatoes

- **Started in 1947**
- **Today, the CTGA is involved in every phase of the state's processing tomato industry, from establishing a fair price to involvement with international trade, and assisting growers with all aspects of their production and marketing.**
- **Mission: The CTGA is an association of California processing tomato growers that provides economic, public policy and business leadership for the benefit of growers and the industry. The Association represents grower interests through services to its members including bargaining, communications and advocacy to ensure the stability, viability and prosperity of the industry.**

Let us now talk a little bit about the CTGA because I think this has relevance to what we need to do in India today. The CTGA was started in 1947. They are involved in assisting growers with establishing a fair price for their produce and help them with all aspects of better agronomy for their production. And also help them with marketing of the produce. What they do is that before sowing, develop a tripartite agreement between the Grower's Association, the farmer and the processor. They know in which area which hybrid does well and they help the farmers to choose the right hybrid. Then they help the farmer with information about the right agronomy. University of California, Davis has Agronomy Extension Advisors who go round the entire California state and help farmers to identify their problems and help them with IPM and other strategies to manage the problems. So, the mission for CTGA is to provide economic, public policy and business leadership for the benefit of growers and the industry.

What CTGA Membership Offers

- **Bargaining**: CTGA sets the price and terms for sale for the annual crop delivery. Grower support gives the CTGA the strength to successfully meet its goals, year in and year out.
- **Communication**: The CTGA keeps growers up to date on issues that affect the farming business through meetings, newsletters and special correspondence.
- **Promotion** : In 2006 formed Tomato Products Wellness Council. TPWC's mission: "To increase the consumption of processed tomatoes through facilitation of pertinent collaborative research and generic communication."
- **Food Safety**: CTGA helps growers explore alternatives such as integrated pest management techniques.
- **Advocacy**: The CTGA actively lobbies to protect growers' interests in the areas of water, labor, pesticides, taxation, transportation, trade and land use.
- **Quality**: The CTGA's original charter mission was to ensure a fair and impartial grading system. For this reason, the CTGA worked to form the California Processing Tomato Advisory Board
- **Research:** In conjunction with the California Tomato Research Institute and private and public researches, the CTGA supports and assists with a broad range of tomato-related research efforts. This research gives the grower the edge to produce a tomato crop second to none.

CTGA provides the seven pillars of support to its members - (1) they bargain for the right prices, (2) they help with communication to help the farmers to keep updated on the business aspects through meetings, etc., (3) they help in promotion of the products through the Tomato Product Wellness Council, (4) they help in food safety measures and management techniques, (4) they help in advocacy to protect farmer's interests because farmers are only two percent of the total membership. The Association helps the farmers who may need to go sometimes to Washington for resolution of certain problems that they face, for taxation, transportation, trade and land use, etc. One of the things Jack Hanna said is that the farmers used to core these tomatoes before processing and this removal of core was getting more labour intensive & hence escalating the cost. The variety they grew hardly had a core and CGTA helped by going to Washington and got the law changed to accept that removing the core is not necessary if the core is below a particular size in millimetres. We need this kind of professional expertise for farmers in India too if we want to get the processing industry to grow in India. (5) they help to measure the quality of tomatoes from the samples which they deliver to the factory and make sure that the quality is maintained by the farmers so that the processors are bound to give them the committed prices based on TSS, viscosity, acidity, etc. as per the contract terms. Tomato trucks first go through the sampling stage at designated stations before going to the factory. The automatic sampler samples the produce in each bin behind the tractors and within about 15 minutes results of the sample for acidity, sugar, viscosity and colour goes to the processor based on which they determine the price. By the time the tractor reaches the factory they have the results of the test on hand. And, (6) they help in making research projects with the breeders in the private sector and as well as for trait breeding in the government institutions.

Top Processing Tomato Groups by Country

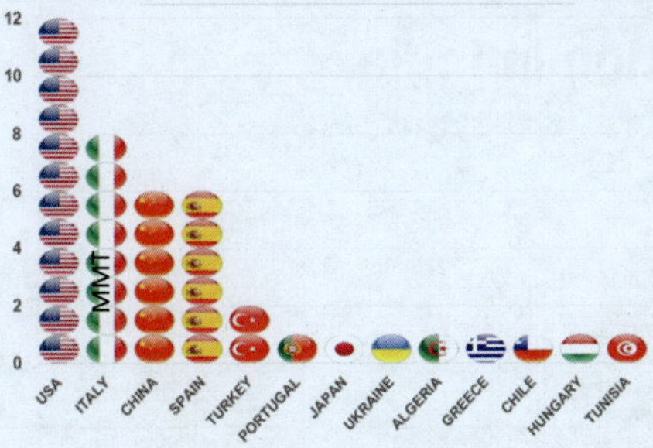

SN	Name of the company	Tomato processed	location	brand
1	Hindustan Unilever	(40,000 tonnes per year) (2011) Now most of the requirement is fulfilled by Varun Agro industries	Nashik Maharastra	Kissan
2	Field Fresh Foods / Del Monte	Products: ketchup and sauces (Quantity Data Not Available)	Krishnagiri, Tamil Nadu	Del Monte
3	Nestle India	Ketchup (Quantity Data Not Available)	Bicholim Goa	Maggi
4	Global Green	ketchup, pasta sauce, tomato blend and pizza sauce. (20,000 tonnes per year)	Srini Food Park in Chitoor, Andhra Pradesh	Tify
5	Indira Foods	tomato ketchup (30 tonnes per day)	Bengaluru	Indira's, Splitz, 2 minutes, Pingani
6	Cremica Group	Tomato Paste and Puree (700 tonnes per Day)	Una in Himachal Pradesh	Cremica squeasy, Tombo
7	Dabur India	Tomato paste & puree (Quantity Not Available)	Siliguri (West Bengal)	Dabur Hommade
8	Capricorn Food Products	Tomato paste and Puree. (100 tonnes per Day)	paste making in Nashik (Maharashtra) and puree production in Koyna (Maharashtra), Krishnagiri (Tamil Nadu), Chitoor (Andhra Pradesh)	supplies paste and puree to leading processors and private labels
9	Nijjer Agro Foods	Tomato paste & puree (Quantity Not Available)	Amritsar	Supplies to Nestle, Del Monte and other processed food makers in the northern Indian region.
10	CD Foods	Tomato Paste and Ketchup (42,000 tonnes per year)	Tarn Taran (Punjab)	Tops
11	Mother Dairy	Tomato Paste and Ketchup (23,000 tonnes per year)	Bengaluru	Safal
12	Godrej Beverages and Foods	Tomato Paste, Puree and Sauce (Quantity not available)	Mumbai	Smart Cook tomato puree
13	GRG Foods	Data Not Available	Bengaluru	Spego brand of tomato ketchup and Revathi brand of tomato-based powders and mixes for the Southern India market.
14	Griffith Laboratories	manufacturers Indian paste and powder mixes (Quantity not available)	Bengaluru	Supply to food services institutional clients
15	Chordia Food Products	Ketchup (2.5 tonnes per day)	Shirwal close to Pune (Maharashtra) and Chennai and Dharwad (Karnataka)	Navin, Toofan
16	Sun-Sip Foods	Tomato Crush, Puree, Paste & (600 tonnes per day (Kolar))	Sunsip Agro Processors, Karnataka & Madanapalle, Chittor Dist, AP.	Sun SIP Tomato Crush
17	Sahyadri Farms	Tomato Puree & Tomato Ketchup (55,000 tonnes per year)	Factory : Dindori, Nashik - 422207, Maharashtra	Sahyadri Farms Tomato Ketchup

According to WPTC (2019), of the 40 tomato processing groups ranked at the **top 12 are based in the USA**, eight in Italy, six each in China and Spain, two in Turkey and one each in Portugal, Japan, Ukraine, Algeria, Greece, Chile, Hungary and Tunisia (Table 6; Figure 3). Morning Star, which has 3 factories in California, has the highest processing capacity of 59000 tons per day. 17 groups in India now

We can see in this slide that India is not among the top countries producing processed tomatoes. USA, Italy, China, and Spain are the top countries. Each of these countries have twelve, eight, six or seven processing groups. In India, we already have 17 processing companies but on a smaller scale and we are only processing about 150,000 tonnes of tomatoes. So, we need our country to go into more breeding of specific varieties/hybrids for processing which will immensely help the processing industry in our country.

Tomato Area & Yield Trend Comparisons 1990 - 2018

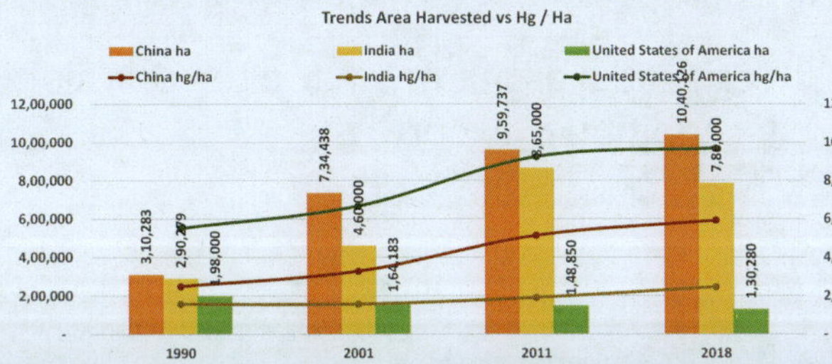

- India at 24.5 t/ha avg yields ½ of China & ¼ of USA, though best farmers 80-100 t/ha
- Area today is nearly 2.5 times more than 90's & yield gains 2.7 times
- Bigger yield gains 2001_2020 due hybrids over 95%
- Area has started to decline as yields increased – last decade
- USA supplies 30% of global processing tomatoes from 1/4th area

The Indian scenario is that, compared to China and the USA, we are half of China and one fourth of the USA in terms of productivity. Area grown today is nearly 2.5 times since 1990 and the yield gains are about 2.7 times. We can also see that bigger gains came after introduction of hybrids (shown in a later slide). Area has started to decline now and it is not going to be growing more than at 2 to 3 percent annually as I think it is already plateauing. The USA produces and supplies 30 percent of the global processed tomatoes.

Current Status of Production in India

- AP,KA highest Yld & prodtn
- MP, Odisha Highest Area low yld
- Top 5 states produce 50% of total
- Mahrashtra ylds surprisngly low
  - Kharif & high summer cultivation ??

Why low avg yields?

- Knowledge deficit at farm level
- Inadequate extension

Rank		Area 000 ha	% of Total		Prodtn. 000MT	% Total Prodn		Yield/ha
1	MADHYA PRADESH	94,5	12%	ANDHRA PRADESH	2.809	13%	ANDHRA PRADESH	46,0
2	ODISHA	82,7	10%	KARNATAKA	2.740	13%	KARNATAKA	43,9
3	CHHATTISGARH	64,6	8%	MADHYA PRADESH	2.737	13%	HIMACHAL PRADESH	40,2
4	KARNATAKA	62,5	8%	TAMIL NADU	1.592	8%	UTTAR PRADESH	39,6
5	ANDHRA PRADESH	61,1	8%	GUJARAT	1.427	7%	TRIPURA	31,1
6	WEST BENGAL	57,7	7%	WEST BENGAL	1.271	6%	TAMIL NADU	30,1
7	TAMIL NADU	52,9	7%	ODISHA	1.206	6%	MADHYA PRADESH	29,0
8	BIHAR	52,2	6%	CHHATTISGARH	1.199	6%	GUJARAT	28,7
9	GUJARAT	49,7	6%	MAHARASHTRA	1.040	5%	PUNJAB	25,0
10	MAHARASHTRA	43,0	5%	BIHAR	964	5%	JAMMU & KASHMIR	24,3
11	TELANGANA	37,6	5%	TELANGANA	878	4%	MAHARASHTRA	24,2
	Total	813,06	81%	Total	21.195	84%	Avg India	26,07

Gains of research not evenly sperad across the country

Regarding the current status of production in India, the top states by area cultivated are different from those with top average yields. We have this mismatch because the type of varieties grown, resources and agronomic expertise among the farmers in different states is vastly different. We need to spread out the benefits of research on larger and relevant areas through deeper knowledge transfer activities. A skilled extension army is required.

India 2nd highest Veg Producer but not in top ten on value addition & Export

Tomato is the major part of value addition for expors

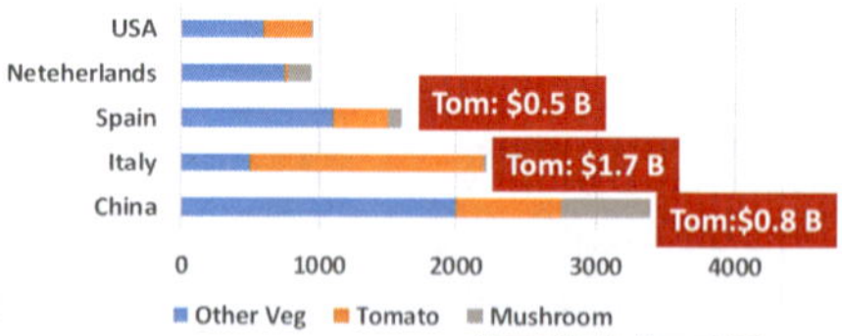

Source: Rabo Bank Report 2017

- **India Processes 1% of total**
- **Processing Seed val $0.5 m today**
- **Tomato biggest opportunity**
- **Today only 7700 ha 1.0%**

Year	Processing Tomato Output mt	Avg yield t/ha	Tot ha grown (process)	Processing Seed Value $ m	Total Tomato Seed Val $ m	Proc ac vs total	Total Area. ha	*Total Prodtn mt*	% Processed
2015	130.000	22	5.909	0,276	33,3	1,2%	500.000	11.000.000	1%
2020	200.000	26	7.692	0,462	44,0	1,0%	770.000	20.020.000	1%

Total Seed value for processing inadequate currently

On the processing and value addition front, we are nowhere in the top 10 countries as we can see in this slide. China has 0.8 billion worth of tomato for processing & export but we import paste annually. This is where we need to increase our processing capacities quickly.

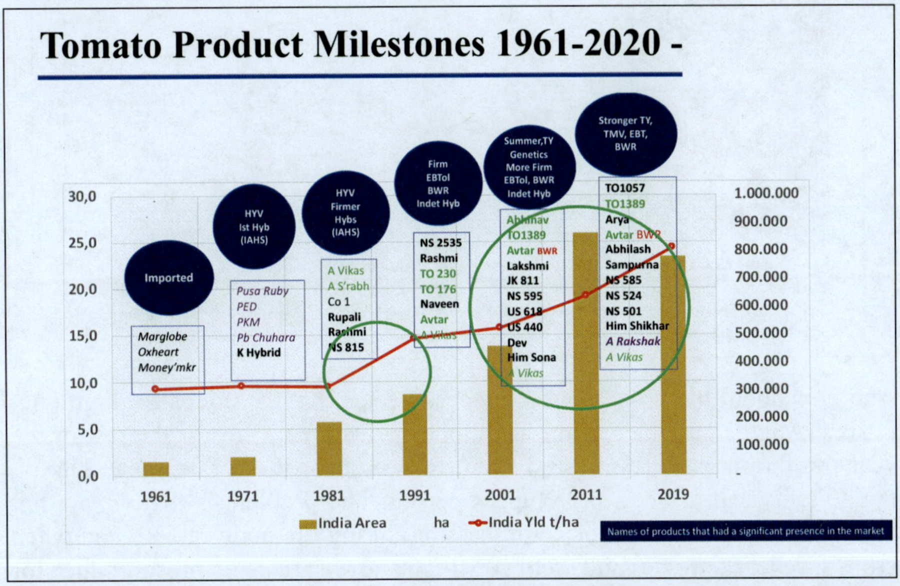

The two circles in the slide show how hybrids from 1980-8, when the first hybrids Rupali & Rashmi were released to the market, have converted the market from open-pollinated varieties to hybrids. And by 2001 to 2011, when Ty genes, genetics for firmness, tolerance to BW, or indeterminate trait, and other beneficial traits were introduced into new hybrids (as shown in blue circles). These are the hybrids that came into the Indian market from different private sector companies. Hence, the average yield of hybrids increased. However, I think, the benefit of higher yield potential of the new hybrids was not spread across all the tomato growing areas. That is why although some farmers get 70 tonnes per hectare yields, the Indian average yields is only 25 tonnes per hectare.

Average Tomato Prices over 5 years

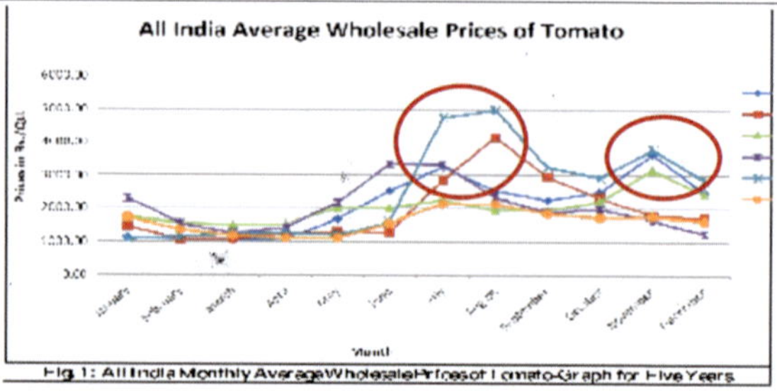

Fig 1: All India Monthly Average Wholesale Prices of Tomato-Graph for Five Years

- **Price Rise is a challenge – June to August & Oct, Nov every year**
- **June – August harvests are of fruits setting in April-June – High Temp & unseasonal rains**
- **Oct –Nov harvests are for fruit set in July/August – High rainfall, humidity & high temp**

And now about the processing tomatoes, we see that the prices are high only in June-August and later again in October-November. But, for the rest of the year the farmers get less than 5 to 10 Rupees per kilo at farm gate. During the 80's, it used to be 2 to 3 Rupees per kg. The problem is that we are not diverting enough production to processing during the main rabi season when crops face least stresses and yield very high and we are using most produce for the fresh market only. We need to move significant portions of November to May harvests to processing for which farmers must get at least 5 to 5.5 Rupees a kilo. But in the processing industry, I think, processors are not willing at the moment to give more than 4 or 5 Rupees per kg. Also, I think we need to increase the average yield by better agronomy because superior genetics already exists so that they can get fair returns for their investment.

Key Traits of Interest for Processing Tomatoes

Gene	Locus Name	Allele	Allele Name	Synonyms	Phenotype	Notes
j	jointless	--		*lf*	The normal pedicel joint, with swelling and abscission layer is absent; fruits separate at the juncture with the calyx; leafy or indeterminate growth of the inflorescence, suppressed in combination with sp (self-pruning).	
j	jointless	+			Normal, jointed pedicels – cracking pleotropic	
j-2	jointless-2	--		*j2*	Jointless elongate pedicel; proliferated inflorescence; elongate fruit.	
sp	self-pruning	--			Plant habit determinate; the position of the inflorescences varies greatly within and between plants in respect to whether they recur every internode or every second internode; plants cover a much smaller space than do normal ones, but cover it more dense	In combination with j, inflorescences are not leafy.
u	uniform ripening	--		*ul*	Unripe fruits of uniform light green color, lacking normal darker shoulder; entire coloration of immature fruit somewhat lighter.	

Now coming to traits, the jointless gene, as I said, helps moving the fruit away from the pedicel by shaking and especially the j2 gene was the one where there was not much of pleiotropic effects like cracking etc., hence that is the gene used in breeding. The self-pruning types do not allow the plant to grow tall like the indeterminate types and prunes itself. It kind of hugs to the ground and keeps the dichotomous branches. They also exhibit an almost concentrated flowering pattern. There is also the uniform ripening type, where there is no green shoulder so that a uniform red colour occurs on the ripe tomato fruit. In the self-pruning gene, we need a determinate plant which can help to get concentrated fruit maturity due to their concentrated flowering which comes from the relatively dwarfing genetics.

These genes combined with the determinate type have led to the non-stake type cultivars that don't need any staking. Especially in North India, e.g., in Ludhiana and other places, some fields are non-staked. Also, in some parts of Bihar where they normally carry out multiple harvests, developing varieties/hybrids with these plant types is critical for the processing industry as growing without stakes reduces cost of cultivation & hence less cost per kg of harvest.

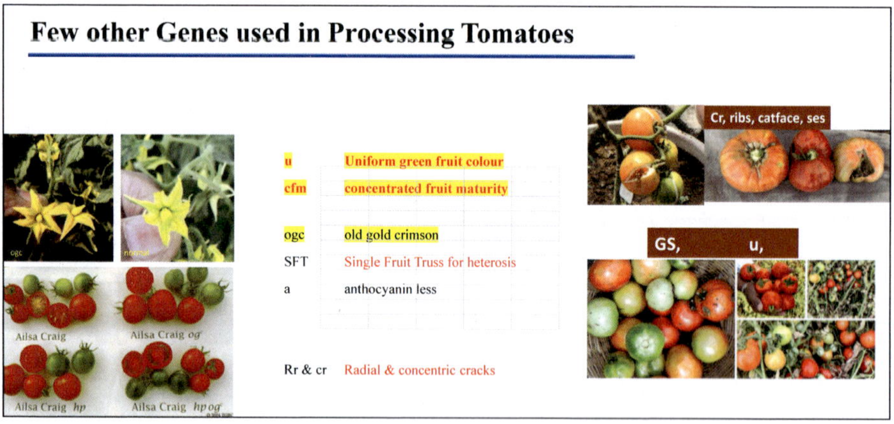

A few other genes that have been used in breeding of processing tomatoes are old gold crimson gene (ogc) which improves the colour of tomato fruits. Single fruit truss (SFT) for heterosis has been recently talked about in Israel by Dr Dani Zamir. It appears to be a single gene that increases yield. The radial (Rr) and resistance to concentric cracks (Cr) genes are equally important to improve physical fruit quality. Cracked fruits invite pathogens & cause fruit rotting. Their inheritance is intermediate and hence both parents need to have Rr & Cr resistance for best results.

Firmness Inheritance & Impact on Breeding

- 0.97 kg/cm2 and 2.66 kg/cm2 in **Parents,**
- 0.83 kg/cm2 to 2.27 kg/cm2 in **F1 hybrids**.
- **inheritance intermediate (6 F1 combinations) & partial dominance of soft parents (5 F1 combinations).**
- **Additive variance component was higher than dominant variance component (0.047/0.026).**
- **Heritability in broad sense** has been **70.7** and **45.7 one in narrow sense**.
- Significant **GCA in 4 lines** & **SCA in 4 F1 hybrids**
- +ve heterosis for firm tomato fruits in 2 F1 tomato hybrids.

Markovic, Z.; Zdravkovic, J.; Damjanovic, M. (Institut za istrazivanja u poljoprivredi "Srbija", Smederevska Palanka (Yugoslavia). Centar za povrtarstvo); 1994

Best to have Firmness on both sides

If we want a good firm tomato, either fresh-market type or processing type, we need both the parents to have firmness to make the hybrids firm. As firmness in the fruit comes from alcohol insoluble solids, e.g., lignins and cellulose, etc., these need to be more to make the fruits firm. They help in slowing the ripening process during which ethylene is produced which in turn makes the fruits softer. Low polygalacturonase enzyme activity reduces the degradation of the tomatoes. So, we need low ethylene production in these kinds of tomatoes.

Root Knot Nematode Resistance

Many cultivars have following combinations today

- **S peruvianum source**
- V, F2, Ty, SW5, N, TMV
- V,F2, TMV, TY, BWR, EB
- V, F2, F3, TY, EB
- Etc etc

- **Markers based on Gel Electrophoresis in 80's**
- **Mi2 linked to Prx 10**

Root knot nematode resistance trait is one of the first ones to be bred in tomatoes using markers with the help of gel electrophoresis in the '80s. I have seen this in Peto Seeds in 1982, California (later Monsanto & now Bayer) where they were using gel electrophoresis to select for Mi2 based on its tight linkage with Peroxidase 10 (Prx10) which is located on chromosome 6. Today SNP markers help do this in a much more efficient way

TMV

Tobacco Mosaic virus symptoms on a tomato seedling

Tomato varieties resistant to ToMV and TMV

To MV Resistant	TMV Resistant	Resistant to both	Resistant Rootstock
Bolseno	Big Beef	BHN-444	Estamino (ToMV)
Tomimaru Muchoo	Celebrity	Health Kick	DRO138TX (ToMV)
Pink Wonder	BHN-871	Sophya	Colossus (TMV)
Beorange	Clermont	Talladega	Maxifort (TMV)
Pozzano	Geronimo		SuperNatural (TMV)
Sunpeach	Sungold		RST-04-105-T (TMV)

Most commonly used gene is Tm2[a] linked to a gene (anthocyaninless)

Then, of course, there is the Tm2a gene that is linked with the anthocyaninless gene which we can recognize even at the seedling stage. It was very easy in the earlier days when we did not have access to the molecular markers to select for this gene before transplanting because the hypocotyl & stems were totally green. We could combine these genes and get TMV tolerance into the Ty and bacterial wilt resistance background. AVRDC (now World Vegetable Centre -WVC), Taiwan have used this gene very effectively to give multiple disease resistant lines to the industry. AVRDC source lines originated mostly from Asheville, North Carolina, USA. I think we too were using them in Pioneer and I think IARI has used them in their breeding programs. Dr Sadashiva, at IIHR, has lots of lines and hybrids that have EB and bacterial blight resistance. These traits have been used to develop varieties that can withstand the fungal diseases and as a result we can save tomatoes from yield losses from these diseases and get more yield per unit area.

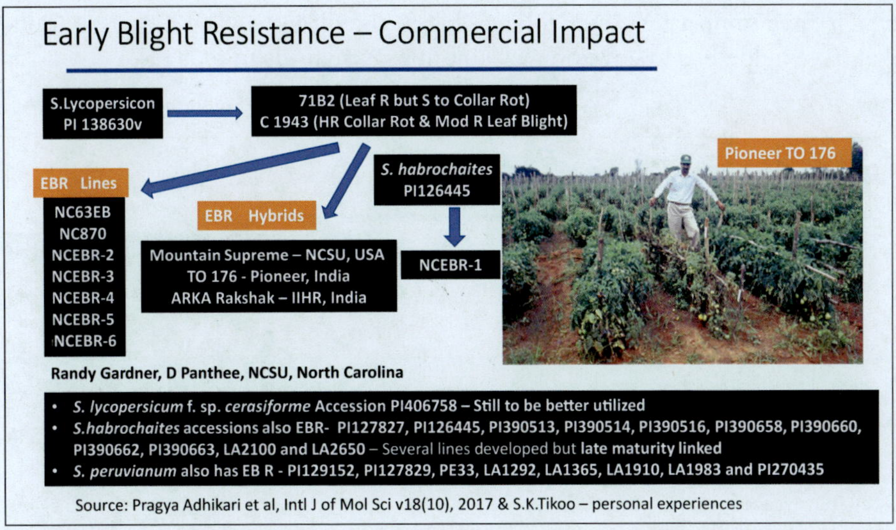

During my work at Pioneer, I was able to utilize the early blight resistance in the EBR lines released from North Carolina State University, Ashville, NC, USA and breed the first EB tolerant commercial hybrid, viz., LIHB0176 (seen here in a demo plot with a susceptible check in between). Dr Randy Gardner and his team bred a series of early blight resistant lines from crosses of a *S.lycopersicon* line with 71B2 and C1943, as also a line EBR from a cross with *S. habrochaites* line PI126445 (Pragya Adhikari et al (2017)). Several hybrids were also developed using these lines in different programs as is shown in the slide.

Based on further work over the years, the situation today is that we have early blight and Ty resistant hybrids (on the left) and susceptible ones on the right, which have almost lost their foliage due to the diseases. These are the traits that have helped us to develop resistant lines & hybrids of today

Bacterial Wilt Resistance

- Bacterial Wilt (*Ralstonia solanacearum*)
- A global challenge
- Sources of resistance
  - H7996, H7998
  - V 48
  - CRA 66 Sel A
- Inheritance (S.K.Tikoo, N Anand, Ram Kishun, 1983, Nirmala Devi & S.K.Tikoo,1991)
  - Incomplete Dominance – BWR1
  - Polygenic recessive – CRA 66 Sel A

Budenhagen & Mohan, 1968, Gilbert et al. 1974, Henderson and Jenkins, 1972, Prior et al. 1994), Tikoo & Anand, 1988, Nirmala Devi , 1986

Now both IIHR & WVC have this in their BW processing lines

The other important trait that has now been incorporated into superior germplasm, especially at IIHR and at WVC, Taiwan is bacterial wilt resistance. Bacterial wilt is a global challenge and the sources of resistance comes from the Hawaii-origin lines like (H series, V48 etc) or the French West Indies line CRA 66 Sel A. S.K.Tikoo et al (1983) and Nirmala Devi & S.K.Tikoo (1991) reported incomplete dominance in a source that can be traced to Hawaii lines and polygenic recessive inheritance in CRA 66-Sel A. Today at WVC, Taiwan, ICAR-IIHR and many other centres around the world the BW genetics has been combined with resistance to TLCV (Tomato Leaf Curl Virus) and both lines and hybrids are now available.

Bacterial Wilt Resistant Releases in India

- IIHR : Arka Abha, Arka Abhijit, Arka Alok, Arka Shreshta, Arka Ananya (ToLCV + BW), Arka Rakshak (ToLCV+BW+Early blight), Arka Samrat (ToLCV+BW+Early blight)
- UAS, Dharwad : Megha
- KAU : Anaga, Shakti, Mukti and Vellayani Viiji
- Orissa Agriculture University and Technology : Utkal Pallavi (BT-1) , Utkal Kumari (BT10), Utkal Deepti (BT-2) etc.
- Pvt Sector: Pioneer (Now BASF): Sun 7711 in 1997 , the first Pvt Sector BW Hybrid (Indeterminate, firm, plum shaped hybrid, still selling in BW affected areas where Indeterminates are grown (Hills)

Processing with BW & TY releases from IIHR & WVC – see later

I have worked on bacterial wilt resistance along with my PhD students. We got our first bacterial wilt resistant varieties, BWR1 and BWR5, from that work. Later I was able to produce a hybrid in Pioneer which was called Avatar 7711, which was the first commercial bacterial wilt resistant hybrid in India. It has good firmness and I think such genetic material can still be used for developing processing tomatoes. There are many bacterial wilt resistant materials released by IIHR, UAS, KAU, Orissa Agricultural University and private sector and some of them have traits that can be utilised to develop processing type hybrids.

Bacterial Leaf Spot

- A global problem of hot & humid regions
- Resistance isolated for various races T1 to T4
- Resistant sources from ***S. lycopersicon*** cerasiforme & ***S. pimpilifollium***
- A broad spectrum source (BSR) in PI 11490 is reported and a QTL on Chrom 11 reported to be linked to resistance to several races but other loci involved too as it confers only 11 to 63 % R
- FL8233, FL8517, and FL8326 developed BSR to multiple races
- Best BSR reported by transgenic method (Bs2 gene from Pepper)

Progress in Developing Bacterial Spot Resistance in Tomato
Sadikshya Sharma and Krishna Bhattarai *
Institute of Food and Agricultural Sciences-Gulf Coast Research and Education Center, University of Florida, 14625 County Road 672,Wimauma, FL 33598, USA; sadikshyasharma@ufl.edu
* Correspondence: krishnabhattarai@ufl.edu; Tel.: +1-813-245-0357

As we go for more and more extended sowing season, we will need bacterial spot resistance as well, especially during the wet seasons. This genetics is also available in the archives of genetic material coming from Florida University and I am sure these can be utilized for producing superior resistant lines. Those interested in this work are referred to krishnabhattarai@ufl.edu who has worked extensively on this disease in University of Florida, USA.

TY – From Adult Plant Resistance to Genetic Resistance

- Genetic studies have led to the mapping of five TYLCV resistance/tolerance genes which are being exploited for resistance breeding. These genes have different origins: *Ty-2* was introgressed from *S. habrochaites*, *Ty-5* (*ty-5*) was introgressed from *S. peruvianum* while *Ty-1*, *Ty-3* and *Ty-4* all originated from different *S. chilense* accessions .

This is how TYLCV expressed itself in 1997 in our seedling inoculation & screening. Avinash was released by Syngenta and Selection 22 was a major OP variety at that time. We can see that at juvenile stage Avinash was definitely vigorous but did not have very high levels of actual tolerance to TYLCV as it did not have Ty genes but had what is called adult plant resistance. Today a series of Ty genes are transferred to commercial hybrids around the world suitable for fresh and processing tomatoes.

Ty Genes Brief Summary

Gene	Chrom	Origin	Trait/Marker Discovery	Refer	Remarks
Ty 1	6	S.chinesis, LA1969	U Fla, Faculty	Ji et al., 2007b; Zamir et al., 1994	2 modifier genes on Chr 3 & 7
Ty 2	11	S.habrochaites, B6013	HAU & WVC	Kalloo & Bannerji 1997 & Hanson et al, 2000	Discovered in Hissar, Bipartite but better against monopartite
Ty 3	6	S.chinesis, LA 2779, LA 1932	U Fla	U Fla, Agrama and Scott, 2006; Ji et al., 2007a	
Ty 4	3	S.chinesis, LA 1932	U Fla	de Castro et al., 2007; Garcia et al., 2007; Ji et al., 2007c; Ji et al., 2009	Smaller effect, recessive, Markers JB-1, T0302, P6–25, and can be used to effectively tagC2_At4g17300 Ty-1 though Ty-4 loci
Ty 5	4	FLA456 (probably derived from Tyking	WVC, UoFla	Kadirvel et al, J Scot et al	Is a loss-of-function mutant allele of the pelota gene (T to G transversion) , recessive
Ty 6	10	Fla. 8638B and Fla. 8472	U Fla,	U Gill, J Scot et al	Ty 6 & Ty 3 homozygotes give highest R for TYLCV & ToMoV in Florida

Pyramiding *Ty-1/Ty-3, Ty-2, ty-5 and ty-6* genes into tomato hybrid to develop resistance against tomato leaf curl viruses and recurrent parent genome recovery by ddRAD sequencing method
•Pardhasaradhi Prabhandakavi, Rambabu Pogiri, Rakesh Kumar, Santanu Acharya, Ramchandran Esakky, M. Chakraborty, Rajasekhar Pinnamaneni & Sairam Reddy Palicherla
Journal of Plant Biochemistry and Biotechnology (2020)

Today there are at least two to three Ty genes, e.g., Ty2, Ty3, available in tomatoes that are offering full resistance in tomatoes to TYLCV. The origin of the Ty genes are summarised in the above slide along with references.

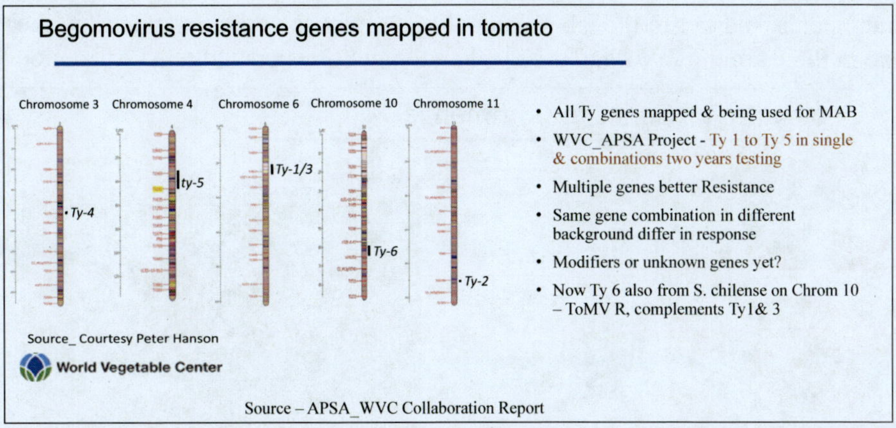

There are six Ty genes known to be distributed on specific locations on chromosomes 3, 4, 6, 10 and 11. Especially the Ty6 gene is now being deployed at Florida University giving some excellent results. We need to utilize them in our breeding programs - both in the fresh market and the processing tomato.

Many of the Ty genes have now been deployed in the commercial hybrids in the market. The below slide which I got courtesy Bob Mullins (APAC Business Lead, Syngenta) in 2010 depicts the deployment of Ty genes through marker assisted breeding at Syngenta, a program that I was involved as the APAC Product Development Lead till 2008. Abhinav was a benchmark in the Tomato industry in India, at that time, not only for firmness but also for TYLCV resistance. It was also better for heat tolerance. So, it created the summer segment where it replaced Avinash. Ty gene in this hybrid was monitored with a molecular marker in the lab at Pune. I had established the molecular marker lab in Pune around 2001 and it served all tomato breeders in the APAC region.

Deploying TY Genes to Commercial

Molecular Assisted Breeding for TY

That work delivered many markers as a breeding aid to the breeders in India. Today IARI, IIHR, IIVR and other institutions are all using these genes in tomato breeding using marker assisted breeding.

Can we create a 25% Processing Tomato situation by 2030

- **Organic Growth and no change or**
- **Take a Goal & achieve it – backward planning**

Year	Processing Tomato Output mt	Avg yield t/ha	Tot ha grown (process)	Processing Seed Value $ m	Total Tomato Seed Val $ m	Proc ac vs total	Total Area. ha	*Total Prodtn mt*	% Processed
2025	500.000	30	16.667	1,111	53,3	2,4%	700.000	21.000.000	2%
2030	7.500.000	40	187.500	12,500	53,3	26,8%	700.000	28.000.000	27%

This means seed value will be 106 cr

How do we move from the current about 2 percent to 25 percent tomato production being utilized for processing in India by 2030? This slide is my take on what to do to achieve that position by 2030. We need to increase the current area with processed tomatoes from about 16,000 ha to 187,000 ha out of the total 750,000 ha under tomatoes. This means that we can then increase the total value of seeds needed for processing type tomatoes from the current approximate value of 9.3 Cr to 106 Cr ($1.1m to $12 m). I think the seed industry will then find it economical to breed for processing type tomatoes because current market values do not allow research investment to go into breeding specifically for processing traits. Hence, the percentage of processing type tomatoes grown will have to go up from the current 2.4 percent to about 26.8 percent and, then, like in other countries, take it up to 50 to 60 percent in the next decade or so. This would mean around 166 crores rupees of seed value in 2040 which means it is a research investment worth doing today by the private seed sector to create better processing varieties.

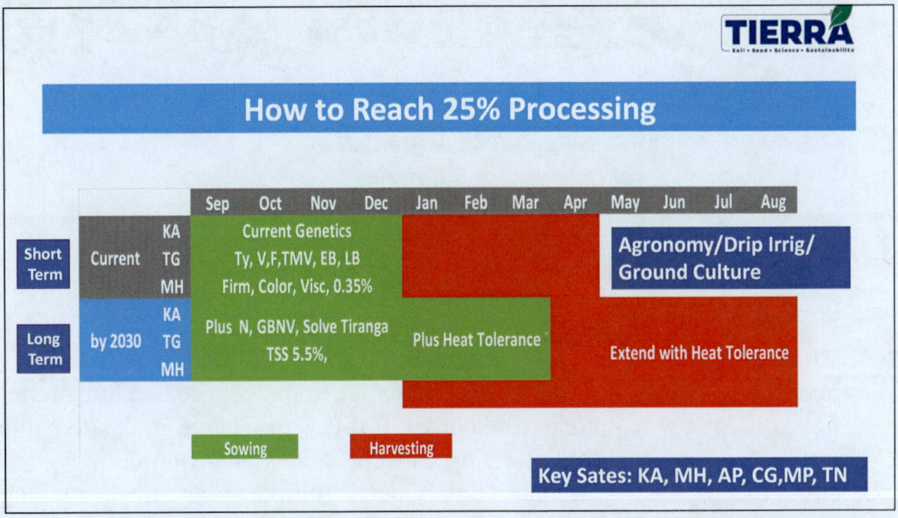

Now, how do we increase to 25 percent processing tomatoes by area? I think there are two ways – in the short term, it is with the current varieties that we have. Basically, sowing happens during September to December, and during January to April harvesting happens, i.e., the red period in the slide. By adopting improved agronomy, drip irrigation and good ground culture (non-staked as staking increases cultivation costs) instead of the current semi-determinate culture may help, because semi-determinate culture means the farmer spends almost about 80-100 thousand rupees per hectare on additional price of staking and labour, while they cannot sell the produce at more than four rupees a kilo to the processors. So, if we reduce the cultivation cost, I think this will help in making cultivation cheaper. Harvesting in January to March is when, as I showed earlier, especially February-March-April the costs are lowest in the market (best season when yield are highest & disease pressures are lowest). This needs a lot of government incentivisation to get farmers trained to meet the requirements of the processing industry. The key states, I feel, where this will be possible are Karnataka, Maharashtra, AP, Chhattisgarh, MP, and TN, because they have large acreages under tomato cultivation and they also have the longest extended sowing seasons. In north India, there is only one sowing season, i.e., sowing in March and they harvest somewhere in June-July-August period and hence not ideal for establishing the processing capabilities.

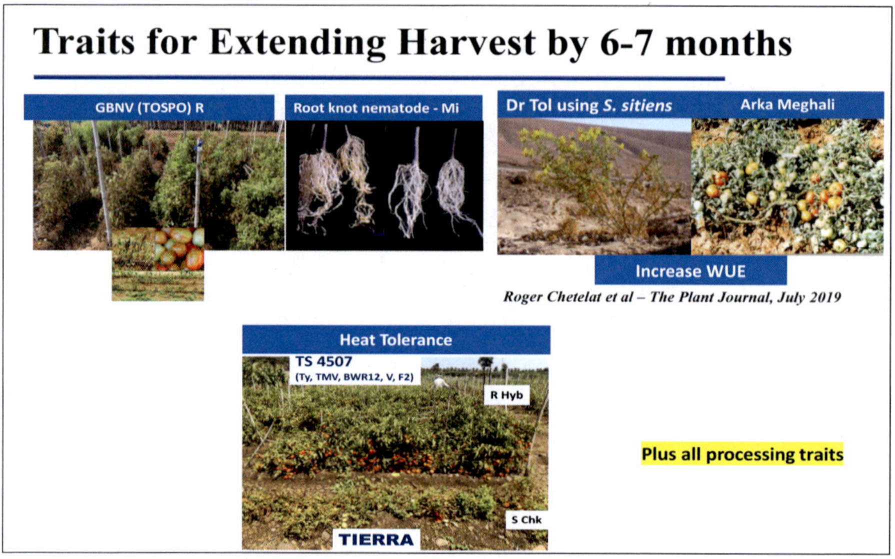

For increasing the area under processing type tomatoes in the long term, we need to breed nematode resistance, TOSPO resistance and solve the *tiranga* problem that is now affecting especially in Maharashtra. *Tiranga* is the effect that is seen on tomato fruits where multiple spots appear making them unmarketable. Studies by IIHR scientists (Dr Krishna Reddy, Personal communication) indicate that three viruses are involved causing this disease, i.e., Tospo (GBNV) transmitted by thrips, TMV (sap transmitted) & Criny Virus (Whitefly transmitted). Resistance to this malady needs to be addressed asap. Also, the TSS (Total Soluble Solids) should be 5.0-5.5 brix value and we can extend the growing season by adding heat tolerance in the hybrids. If we can add heat tolerance, we may have a continuous cropping of tomato that would allow harvest for nine months. Why I am stressing on this aspect is that if we have a nine-month crop, the tomato processing factories don't have to worry about washing the processing machinery and trying to find other crops to process. So, this will make it more efficient in terms of cost of processing for the processing companies as the factory will be idle only for three months in a year. The combined traits that we need in processing tomatoes are GBNV tolerance, root knot nematode tolerance, heat tolerance and maybe drought tolerance in future. Of course, now drought tolerant material is available from IIHR program which I had started long back in the 80's from which a drought tolerant variety Arka Meghali was released later. There is also material being developed in California by Dr Roger Chatelet, who is working on *S. sitiens*, developing drought tolerant material which is in an advanced stage of breeding right now. So, we need to use these genes and to do this successfully we need

PPP kind of arrangements so that we can deliver appropriate material in five to seven years from now.

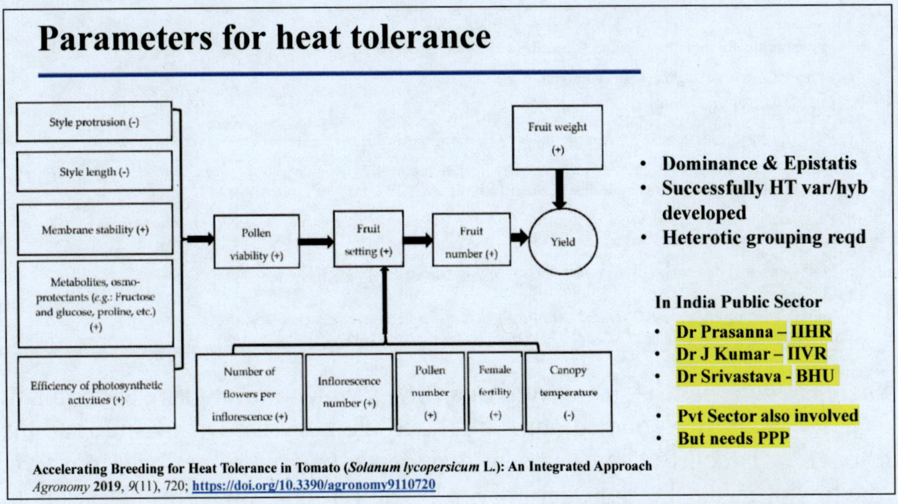

There are many traits which govern heat tolerance - style protrusion, style length, membrane stability, pollen viability, fruit setting, fruit number, number of flowers, etc. There is a research paper which I came across recently on heat tolerance that says that dominance & epistasis control this trait. We can select for this trait in the field. We can use marker assisted breeding for other traits and for heat tolerance, we select in the right hot spot. Thus, we will be able to create good heat tolerant material. There is a need to work on heterotic grouping by including Ty and other genes and heat tolerance. We in India have done excellent work on delivering relatively better heat tolerance already- Hybrids Abhinav, 1057 from Syngenta made the Feb sowing possible in Maharashtra and Karnataka. Dr. Prasanna at IIHR, Dr. J. Kumar at IIVR and Dr. Srivastava at BHU are doing further excellent work in this area to understand the basics of heat tolerance. We should be working with the private sector on PPP mode as we already have hybrids that are sown in February which get harvested in April-May-June. So, we need to work together to extend the crop to harvest at a later date. If we are able to extend the harvesting season beyond June, we will also need to have very high foliage heat tolerance built into this. So, we need a long-term breeding program in processing tomatoes.

SFT – Single Overdominant Gene for Yield

- heterozygosity for tomato loss-of-function alleles of *SINGLE FLOWER TRUSS* (*SFT*),
- which is the genetic originator of the flowering hormone florigen,
- increases yield by up to 60%.
- Yield overdominance from *SFT* heterozygosity is robust, occurring in distinct genetic backgrounds and environments.
- We show that several traits integrate pleiotropically to drive heterosis in a multiplicative manner[2], and these effects derive from a suppression of growth termination mediated by *SELF PRUNING* (*SP*), an antagonist of *SFT*.
- First example of a single overdominant gene for yield and suggests that single heterozygous mutations may improve productivity in other agricultural organisms.
- Works only in +/- heterozygous state when crossed with sp genotypes. Personal experience not confirmed yet

Source: The flowering gene *SINGLE FLOWER TRUSS* drives heterosis for yield in tomato
Uri Krieger, Zachary B Lippman, Dani Zamir, Nature Genetics, 2010, 42, 459-463

There is a gene called 'single fruit truss (SFT)' which is a single over dominant gene for yield. It is sourced out from the SP gene by Dr. Dani Zamir and his team from Israel. But my personal experience so far has not been positive. Maybe not using the right germplasm is the reason. I thought that I should let this audience know about the gene & more work needs to be done to successfully deploy in our conditions. This gene is also available from TGRC.

High TSS Breeding & Flavour

- L. Chmilewski – Rick Sugar Lines with TSS of over 6.5 %
- QTL's at INRA

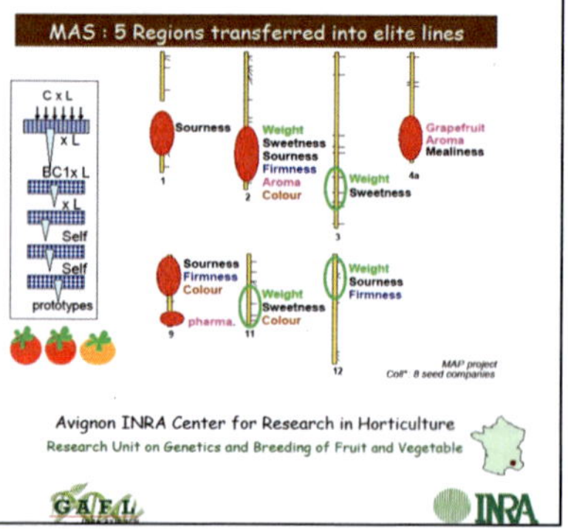

To increase flavour, there are now QTLs available at INRA on sourness, firmness, sweetness, colour, and aroma. There are five QTLs available and one needs to work with INRA. Maybe there are others who have worked on the QTLs. At INRA the first high sugar line, from *L. chmilewiski* was developed which had a TSS of 16 per cent. Rick TSS lines were developed by Charlie Rick with a TSS of over 6.5 percent. These are available at TGRC. Improving the sugar content involves a lot of work because as the TSS levels increase the yield reduces. One needs to do a lot of work to get to that average 5.5 to 6 percent TSS in the firm processing type tomatoes that are needed in once-over harvest.

Processing Tomato Breeding IIHR– BW & TY

Avika Apeksha

Arka Vishesh

Exploited processing qualities such as jointless gene and CFM. ICAR-IIHR released Var Sel 11 in 1987 & two high yielding F_1 hybrids,2019 *viz,* **Arka Apeksha and Arka Vishesh** suitable for processing & yiled of 75 -80 t/ha. Processors - Sunsip Foods, Karnataka; Sahyadri Food Processing, Maharashtra; Jaldi Foods, Tamil Nadu; and Cremica Foods, Punjab found both the varieties suitable for processing

The tomato breeding work at IIHR to develop processing tomatoes, besides what I developed in 1987, i.e., selection 11, which I think had jointless gene, two superior hybrids have been developed by Dr. Sadashiva. They are called Arka Apeksha and Arka Vishesh. Processing industry has tested them and they have the potential to produce 75-80 tons per hectare. These hybrids have also been found to meet the industrial requirements for the processing tomatoes.

World Vegetable Centre Breeding – BW & TY genes

Dr Peter Hanson's work: Two dual purpose (fresh market an processing) lines, *viz,* **AVTO 1706 & AVTO 1707** suitable for non-staked cultivation with required fruit quality and yield under open field conditions have been developed by World Vegetable Center (WVC).

Peter Hansen's breeding work at WVC, Taiwan has also led to the development of dual type tomatoes, i.e., for fresh market as well as for processing. There are two varieties, viz., AVTO 1706 and AVTO 1707, which have been found highly suitable for processing. In 2020-2021, there was an initiative by WVC, Taiwan, along with INB Seeds at Bangalore under Mujib and his team. They were kind enough to provide their field for a trial with staked and non-staked tomatoes and they found five to six hybrids and varieties that were good enough for processing. I was glad that one of our hybrids at Tierra, TS 4719, was also found suitable for processing and was one of the highest yielders in the trial. All these varieties and hybrids need to be now taken to large scale testing stage and advanced to commercial so that processing tomatoes become a reality in India.

Processing Tomatoes

Can we create a Heinz in India

- "Catsup" in 1876 in Pittsburgh, Pennsylvania,
- Heinz Tomato Ketchup remains the best selling brand of ketchup.[2][3]
- From 1906 it was produced without preservatives.[4]
- In 1907, Heinz started producing 13 million bottles of ketchup per year, exporting ketchup all over the world, including India, Australia, South America, Japan, Indonesia, New Zealand, South Africa and the United Kingdom.
- Heinz ketchup is often served at restaurants globally - . As a condiment for many foods, such as french fries, chips, hamburgers and hot dogs,
- Heinz ketchup uses the slogan, "America's Favorite Ketchup." As of 2012, there are more than **650 million bottles of Heinz Tomato** Ketchup being sold every year throughout the world.[5]
- In January 2009, the label was replaced with an illustration of a vine-ripened tomato accompanied by the slogan "Upgrade To Heinz".[6]
- In a recent American Customer Satisfaction Index poll of 10,644 consumers, H.J. Heinz Co. had the highest score of any food or beverage firm, higher than Kraft, Coca-Cola, and Nestlé
- **Worlds most famous brand of tomato ketchup – Colour & Viscoscity USP**

My dream is to see that we create a Heinz in India. Why should we take up cultivation of specialized processing tomatoes? When we buy a ketchup bottle from the shelf, if we open the ketchup bottle, it quickly flows out. But if we open the ketchup bottle from recognized companies, like Heinz, where proper processing type tomatoes have been used for processing, it will not flow out that easily and one needs to tap the bottle at the bottom to get that paste out. This is because they have always bred for very high viscosity which is resulting from higher levels of alcohol-insoluble solids (AIS) in their processing tomatoes. Alcohol-insoluble solids improve firmness & viscosity in the tomato. Heinz is the number one brand among the tomato processing companies globally and I think we need to create a Heinz in India by providing all the necessary components - the right varieties, the best agronomy and complete support to the farmers. I feel this is where an FPO system will help.

Similarly, I found recently that Kagome, Japan, (They own United Genetics, which has a branch in India too) have started claiming specific functional advantages of their tomato products. They mentioned that since their products can reduce cholesterol, they are good for health. The company Sana Tech, Japan, have developed a genetically-edited tomato which expresses Gaba protein, has oval-elongated fruits which are suitable for fresh market and processing into juice as well. Gaba protein is known to reduce mental stress in human beings and hence this kind of improvement is needed in India also. Hence these areas of improvement in processing tomatoes - better processing quality, better nutritional quality plus suitability for processing as juice, sauce and ketchup – can help develop a sustainable tomato processing industry in India.

We are not far from what is required today- Need the will

Parameters	Parameter in the existing commercial tomatoes	Parameters desired by Processing Industry
Plant habit	Determinate / Semi-determinate	Determinate
Fruit weight	90-100 g	60-70g
Fruit shape	Oblate / Oblong/ round/Square round /Oval	Round/oval/pear
Fruit firmness	Soft/medium/Firm/ very firm	Firm
Fruit colour	Light red to deep red	Deep red
Pedicel	Jointed / Jointless	Jointless
Fruit shoulder	Uniform green/ green	Uniform green
Fruit maturity	Gradual	Concentrated fruit maturity
Vine storability	For limited period	Prolonged vine storability
TSS (degree brix)	4-4.7	5.5 or higher
Colour value	1.98-2.12	> 1.95
Acidity (%)	0.34-0.38	<0.40
pH	4.21-4.41	< 4.40
Texture/ Firmness (kg/cm^2)	6-8	>8
Lycopene (mg/100g FW)	8-10	>12
Lycopene in tomato paste , 27-28 degree brix (mg/100g FW)	12-14	>14
Viscosity (Botswick, cms/30 sec)	10-12	12-14
Disease resistance	Resistant to ToLCV, BW, V,F,	MDR – ToLCV as basic
Yield (t/ha)	75-80 in best	➢ 75-80

We are not far from what is required today in the processing industry. We need to reduce tomato fruit weight, but we need to get more fruit numbers in a plant. We need deep red fruit colour, jointless gene in all the processing varieties for easy harvest at the ripe stage. We need concentrated fruit maturity, and prolonged vine storability. We need a TSS of 5.5 or more. We need lycopene levels more than 12 grams per 100 grams of fresh weight. We need high viscosity (measured in terms of distance travelled by the paste in 30 seconds which should be more than 14 centimetres). In tomato juice production, when we make juice from a normal tomato, in about half an hour, the serum and the solids separate. When there are more alcohol insoluble solids (AIS) and hence good viscosity, the serum separation happens after a much longer time thereby improving juice quality - means better quality juice and ketchup. In addition, we need multiple disease tolerances – TLCV resistance, fusarium tolerance, verticillium tolerance, foliage tolerance and heat tolerance. Although I said earlier that we have hybrids having 75 to 80 tonnes yield potential per ha, the average productivity in India is only 25 tonnes, and this needs to change. Question is how do we move to reach that target.

Key Lessons

- **Not a Win Win situtaion today**
  - Farmer – Poor Yield/Low Prices/Gluts
  - Processor – Cant pay higher/Product Quality
  - Seed Co – Processing market low priority
- **Majority growers are Small Farmer Holders**
- **Contract Farming not working**
- **Staked culture hence can't sell at low price**
- **Inadequate Knowledge transfer**
- No **proper wide area testing in ground culture** carried out barring WVC intervention

The lessons we have learned is that today it is not a win-win situation. Farmers still are getting poor yields and the processor can't pay higher prices due to low product quality standards for processing. For seed companies, the processing market is still a low priority. Today, the majority of the growers are small farmers with about 1 to 2 acres. Processors are carrying out contract farming but this is not always working because when farmers get better prices, they don't honour the contract. They take their produce to the fresh market. This is a problem that needs to be solved. Staked culture is too expensive. Inadequate knowledge transfer is another problem. There is no proper wide area testing in non-staked ground culture. We need intervention like the trial conducted under the WVC & GIZ together a few years back. We need to do it at an all-India level using the extension machinery. Using the public and private sector partnerships and using KVK locations for testing could be one of them.

Recommendations

- Breeding: HYV MDR processing tomato varieties and F_1 hybrids with CFM, jointless pedicel suitable for once over harvest - with high lycopene and brix of above 5 %.
- Varieties/Hybrids suited to extend growing season to 9 months – **PPP projects**
- Adopting CRISPR/Cas-9 based mutagenic approaches for desired cultivars in less time/improving e.g GABA gene in tomato processing variety **Sicilian Rouge by** Sanatech Seed company, Japan.
- Indian tomato processing sector to look at value-added products, including those for the pharmaceutical and nutraceutical industries. e.g sun dried tomatoes, whole fruit canning
- Greater government support to help develop areas for production – **Karnataka, MH state, MP, CG, AP, TN as longer production seasons possible**
- Growers Association like CTGA – FPO's with CTGA type goals – Strong Extension & professional help on disease & pest control
- Constant Knowledge gaining - Participating in International events - **ISHS symposia** & processing tomato Conferences organized by **WPTC** every 2 years; **Fruit Logistica**

Here are my final recommendations. MDR (Multiple Disease Resistant), high yielding processing tomatoes should be targeted in breeding programs to create concentrated fruit maturity, jointless pedicel, high lycopene content and brix value of above five percent. The variety should be suited for extended growing season or specifically bred for rabi & summer seasons to help create a prolonged sowing window. As I explained earlier, by adopting gene editing technology to get Gaba and other gene mutations, it is possible, just like the Sicilian Rouge tomato produced by Sana Tech, Japan. This will help create value-added products that will cater to a different segment of the consumers. Thereby reducing pressure on prices in the glut season. Also, by using gene editing technology with existing tomatoes, add high-value genes to them, making them better quality tomatoes. Processing sector to look at value-added products including those for which they will be able to pay more for nutraceutical purposes, sun-dried tomatoes, for whole food canning, etc., besides ketchup. In the important tomato-growing states like Karnataka, MP, Chhattisgarh, AP, and TN the local governments need to increase their support to make PPP possible, so that we can do large-scale testing. We need to create our own CTGA (California Tomato Growers Association) like bodies. FPOs is a right direction to emulate CTGA as they can help farmers to take up informed decision based sowing where market linkages are set up before sowing takes place. We do need to brainstorm and make the above recommendations happen. And, to gain constant knowledge from breeding to farming to processing, we need to attend National & International symposia that happen regularly e.g: Indian International Society of Horticultural Science, Processing Tomato World Conference organized by the WPTC, and attend Fruit Logistica, where they honour quality achievers, and one can listen to them and to the latest happening in these fields.

Therefore, in the final analysis, the ground culture will be the key for increasing the processed tomatoes area in India. I have one last submission that we may not be able to get machine harvesting like the one used in California right away in India because our farmer's holdings are very small. In Japan, for tomato harvesting, they have developed harvesters which can operate in just about three to four acres. So, for three to four such farmers there could be one harvester. In the slide on bottom left is Mr. Muniyappa, my assistant in the IIHR fields in the 1980s. We worked on concentrated fruit maturity and jointless gene. We used to shake the plant to get all the fruit off the plant. We had varieties and hybrids with all fruits ripe on the plant which on shaking dropped all fruits into the tray - as shown in the photo. My Ph.D. student Dr. J C Rajput, worked on this aspect, and we were able to harvest them once over. So my idea at that time was, which was also published, that we can grow varieties where one can pick up the whole tomato plant and shake them into a bin, instead of multiple pickings. I think this is the way to ensure the growing of processing tomatoes on a large scale in 10 years. If FPO's work well, mini harvesters can help speed up mechanical harvest in a small way and once the consolidation of such practice grows on a large-scale larger scale mechanical harvesters can be employed in ten years or so.

Acknowledgements

- **Dr A T Sadashiva, Ex Head Veg Crops, ICAR-IIHR**
- **Dr Peter Hanson – Ex Principle Breeder WVC, Taiwan**
- **Dr Bindumadav – Ex WVC, Taiwan**

I would like to acknowledge that some parts of the information in my presentation was shared with me by colleagues in the field - Dr Sadashiva, Dr Peter Hansen and Dr Bindumadav.

Questions and Answers

Dr Partha Das Gupta (Comment): This was a discourse of a very high standard and high value to researchers and other stakeholders. A lot of food for thought has been provided for the policy makers and the industry too. Kudos to ATPBR for organizing this webinar. Of course, to Dr Suren Tikoo who has done full justice to the subject.

Jagadish: Can we restrict the duration of the tomato crop in open field conditions so that we can harvest at 120 to 130 days in north of India. I am particularly talking about UP.

Suren Tikoo: Yes – it is possible to extend the crop's duration in North India including in UP. However, we would need other genetic traits that are not available in the current varieties. These other traits would include resistances for the diseases that may become important due to extending the season. We would need cold tolerance at seedling stage and heat tolerance at the end of the season. However, if we consider MP and south of MP, these states have a longer growing season. The farmers are making more money as they sow in January to March because of which they get at least 20 Rupees per kilo at the farm gate. They are growing as many as 95 or 96 different hybrids that are in the market. OPs are either no longer grown by the farmers, or grown on a very little area. After incorporating the traits, we need to work very hard on having agronomists and engineers to ensure the produce suitable for the processing industry is produced economically and efficiently.

Jagadish: One small query - can we integrate these traits in the rainy season tomato especially for kharif?

Suren Tikoo – The rainy season crop must have wilt resistance, early blight (*Alternaria sp*) as well as late blight (*Phytophthora sp*) resistance, and fruit rot resistance. Those genes are available in genetic material that Cornell University and IIHR have also developed. We need to work together to develop such rainy season tomatoes for processing. I have said this on 6th March, 2023 in an Industry-Public sector seminar at Delhi, chaired by the Director General, ICAR. I hope that some of the points I made will be followed up and acted upon leading to the development of some projects.

Rajeev Taggar – Dr. Tikoo, thank you for an inspiring talk in which I learnt a lot. Thanks to the organizers who have done a very good job. I have two questions. The first one is that when we talk about processing, we notice that ketchup and sauce are very popular abroad but in India consumers prefer to go for fresh tomatoes. Some of the reasons for this lower usage could be due to perceptions on preservatives. What is your take on the issue of preservatives and how to clarify this issue in our minds?

Suren Tikoo - Thank you for your kind words. First, as we cannot grow tomatoes throughout the year, we need to transport them for long distances. Secondly, there is nothing wrong with processing if it is done properly. As I said earlier, lycopene becomes better absorbable if it is heated and processed. Many research studies are there on this aspect which can be found in CGTA that I had referred to. And the third thing is that we are importing more than 25 million dollars' worth of processed tomatoes and in the last three years, in one year alone, there was a 146 percent increase. This means that we do want to consume processed tomatoes. Also, one can discover hundreds of recipes that can be prepared with these various canned tomatoes. About the preservatives, I eat a processed food item which is more like a jam, not made with tomato but with other fruits, and it has no preservatives. They use grape juice as a preservative in this food item. It is a French technology, sold in India and I know that some of them are now using radiation for better preservation. As the demand for such preservation technologies increases which may be enviro-friendly or healthier, they may be free from chemical preservatives. I am not sure if they are really healthier, but their claim is that they are healthier. Kagome is advertising similarly, which is a Japanese company, and that country cares seriously for citizen's health. The Japanese Govt has approved Canotec guava protein which is a GE product besides the already mentioned Gaba Protein containing tomato, also a GE product. There are soft claims on the bottles of Kagome that the products are healthier. Finally, it is the quality of the processing which is important which can overcome the hurdles that you mentioned.

Chattopadhyaya – I am from Bhagalpur, Bihar Agricultural University. Thank you very much for your very informative talk covering nearly all aspects of the processing industry and how to develop it. I would like to add a couple of points. The first one is from one of our experiences regarding breeding. We are running projects on developing tomatoes specifically suited for processing purposes, and we have used one of the genes - a natural mutant allele of ovoid gene. This is a fruit elongation & shape related gene and we have found that this mutant allele is very well correlated with firmness of the fruit. We recommend the use of this ovoid allele mutant for fruit firmness. The second point is regarding promoting tomatoes for processing purposes. We are lacking, at our university, or at our state level, proper PPP approaches. The public sector and private sector should join hands so that we can share the materials between us towards a holistic development. If you kindly suggest some of the practical ways through which we can actually achieve that, it will be very useful.

Suren Tikoo - If there is a gene marker, we could use it, for e.g., if you are crossing an oval square round or an elongated fruit with a round type, then we could select in F2 by using the marker and discard the overweight fruits and select only the oval types. Round types can be rejected based on eye selection and carry these to the field whereas marker usage can be avoided. This means we are increasing selection efficiency by using the markers. No two opinions about that. However, we need to use marker-based selection right at the seedling stage. The second point is about PPP. I have talked enough about the PPP during the just concluded meeting on 6 March 2023 in Delhi. There is a serious attempt on these partnerships directed by the DG. He was very clear that the industry is the fourth pillar without which we cannot help the research results to reach the farmer. Under horticultural sciences, we had some seven to eight action points to focus on for vegetable crops. The main concern is that there has to be trust between the industry and the public sector. We need to improve our understanding by talking more to each other. So, all I can say is that we have to initiate those meetings with the right people from both sectors and decide on what areas we want to work in Bihar and in other parts of the country

Chattopadhyaya – We, from the state government also are having a large initiative regarding protected cultivation and particularly breeding of the processing type tomato lines. The state government has a Krishi road map and we are trying to have this kind of projects and programs focusing mainly on protected cultivation, under which processing type tomatoes are to be developed.

Zakir Hussain - With reference to the comments made earlier by Dr Jagadish, I would like to share one or two of our observations. We have observed that if we are able to concise the flowering time and convert it into fruiting at 23 to 25 degree C temperature range, that will be the most appropriate. So, what is happening in North India is that it starts from the second fortnight of October and the whole of November which results in very high yield. But it requires resistances to bipartite virus. Definitely, Ty3 will be compulsorily needed in the lines, if we really want to enhance the yield. If the yield is not good, then definitely the price issues will be there.

Suren Tikoo - Resistance is certainly required, and we already have those combinations of genes that work. We need to now combine them into all the processing traits I mentioned earlier and get a hybrid ready for all those areas where we need to extend the season. We will need different traits at different times of the season which need to be identified. Then a breeding plan to be prepared to bring together the two parents that will ultimately give the hybrid that we need.

Zakir - The second submission is that the apprehension that we are not having varieties or hybrids suitable for processing purposes, and that we don't have any genetic variability in India are not completely correct. Whatever crop Improvement programs we are doing is with imported germplasm, and a majority of the imported lines are of processing type. So, if we evaluate them, the majority of lines and hybrids are meeting the standards for bricks and acidity levels of the processing types. So, there is no dearth of genetic material for processing types.

Suren Tikoo - Please don't get me wrong. I already mentioned that some of the hybrids, varieties and lines are having the traits suitable for processing, and some processing companies already have confirmed that they have the right traits. So, what we need is to have proper testing only in the ground culture with no staking. This is to reduce the cost of cultivation for the farmer so that he can sell it at the right price. By staking, he cannot sell it at five rupees a kilo. Currently, he is losing money. Materials are available but we need to get them together into a whole package today. As I said in my last slide, we are almost there. However, somewhere something may be missing. Getting all together into a few entities and then testing material like heat tolerance, etc., is needed. Whether it is in the exact processing background or not is the issue. As far as the germplasm material is concerned, material suitable for processing is available freely all over the world. One can access them either from public sector or private sector sources. One can get it from across the world through proper procedures. And, hybrids themselves are a source of germplasm that can be used for breeding purposes and it will take five to six years to get a new desirable hybrid/variety. Finally, it needs good molecular breeding processes, good agronomy to come up with a time-bound project for effective delivery. So, no two questions about what you said that the right genetic materials are available and that we can extend cultivation in north India in September-October sowing and getting to harvest in March by using the right material. And, one would need cold tolerance too in them.

Sharad Deshpande – While in Syngenta, you were developing the hybrids and I was marketing them. The earlier tomato hybrids which came into market were all fleshy and processing types. Suddenly, the seed industry realized the demand for juicy, acidic and sambar types. The new hybrids which came into the market are all green shoulder and acidic in taste. Now you are proposing a push for the processing types. Do you think the Indian market is ready to buy the processed tomatoes? Because, in Karnataka, for example, even at our home also, we don't use any processed tomatoes. Only in the restaurants, we get served such types. Also, we may prefer to use fresh tomatoes. What is your take on this?

Suren Tikoo - I think the study that I referred to was from the National Academy of Science by Dr Mohapatra which has got all these details. We are importing ketchup today. Instead, why not produce our own tomatoes for processing specifically. Secondly, I think it may be that some people don't like to use tomato ketchup, sauce, etc. It is very common in cities and the total requirement is enough to warrant that we breed for processing requirements. The points that Rajiv raised help us to move towards making them relatively healthier by using techniques that don't use more preservatives, don't use more salt, etc. Today methods are available that can help that but not breeding for processing types. I am not saying that everything will move to processing types. What I said is that between February to June when farmers lose money, why not transfer that to processing so that they make the money and people get what they want. That was the point I was making.

Chattopadhyaya - Let me add something here. We had a unique opportunity this time when there was a Regional Kisan Mela at our University. We surveyed around 150 consumers and farmers regarding their preferences in tomatoes. We had some of the different coloured lines – pink, yellow, orange, as well as some of the juicy and fleshy types. We observed that there is also a very good demand not only for the juicy type but also the fleshy type. Based on what the survey indicated, I suggest that the product coming out of processing also has scope for diversification. Apart from ketchup and sauce, we can think of tomato soup or tomato juice. Nowadays a lot of work is being carried out on water soluble tomato concentrates which are being used for medicinal purposes. What is your opinion?

Suren Tikoo - In my recommendations, I have mentioned that we need processors to look at other value-added products, e.g., sun-dried tomatoes, juices and high-flavonoid tomatoes, purple tomatoes, etc. We need to get into value addition so that farmers also earn money but for that value addition, processors and the consumers have to be ready to pay more. For example, I had seen in one of my visits to JusCo Store in Tokyo, two strawberry types available - one with higher soluble solids, and the second an old strawberry variety. The Japanese consumer pays double the price for the first one. Clearly the consumer was ready to pay more for a better tasting variety. As people's purchasing power increases, these trends will definitely emerge in India too. In the Indian markets, we know that there are about 10 crore people who are price agnostic. They need variability and it is a fact that they can buy a kilo of tomato at 200 rupees a kilo if it comes with the right value-added information. Also, they can buy one watermelon for 100 rupees or more because it is seedless. These will happen in the next 10 years and we will see value-added products entering our shelves. In vegetables and fruits like tomatoes too, what happened to apples in India will happen. In 2003, when for the first time, Fuji and Gala apples came in, they were taking only 10 percent shelf space and selling at twice the price. Today they take 90 percent shelf space because consumers understood the quality and understood the value of that. As such products are introduced into the market and branding and communication is carried out properly, such products will get better acceptance.

Sundaraj – It was a very good presentation. You have covered almost everything with statistics. We have to move over to the processing types. Earlier we obtained some germplasm from the U.S. Our country and our population are poor. Our people want around 9 to 10 fruits per kg.. But the type which processing people use to produce ketchup is very costlier than the fresh produce. Also, China is dumping a lot of paste into India at a very low price. Therefore, what is the scope of the processing industry in India? Also, the consumer awareness of using ketchup is very low in our country.

Suren Tikoo - I think consumer awareness is increasing by the day and China's dumping may not continue to happen forever. The processing industry is aware of this. I showed that we already have 17 companies doing tomato processing. They will not just shut shop and go. I think they will finally arrive at a pricing which may be economical to farmers, processors and consumers. The final product will be costly because one bottle of ketchup takes three to four times more tomato to dry and dehydrate to the right stage of consistency in the final product . To make that happen we have to pay more for the ketchup. As it is concentrated, we need just a few drops of ketchup and not the full tomato.

Guru Murthy - Thanks for your nice presentation. I had expected, as a breeder, more breeding-related topics in your presentation. My first question is that in the last 56 years the yield has increased only by 2.7 times. And the price being offered by the processing companies is also less which means that we need to increase the yield further. How much yield increase do we need to increase from now on when the rate of increase is very less?

Suren Tikoo - As I said we have to have better agronomy to reach all farmers. Currently, only a few farmers are producing 70 tonnes per hectare which will not do. Almost every farmer getting 50 tonnes per hectare is needed. Genetically, we can increase the yield by increasing heat tolerance to get more yield during the hot season. And, we need to find new genes, like SFT, and new useful genes from the wild relatives. Because, if you just look at the number of fruits as a trait in pre-breeding work with *S. pimpinilifolium*, we notice that it can produce more than 10 kilos of tomatoes per plant whereas we currently reach about four to five kilos at the most. We also need to have a little more biomass but at the same time for processing it has to be the determinate type because we don't want to spend on staking. So, we need to determine if we need to increase fruit numbers. I think I talked about the required traits in breeding and how they are inherited. Most of the traits I talked about have markers and marker-aided selection can be a separate talk.

Guru Murthy – About the SFT gene, it produces only one or two flowers per plant. So, for a private company, that is a lose-lose situation.

Suren Tikoo - I think if you refer to what Dani Zamir says about SFT in his new paper, you will find that he has developed the material by crossing SFT with several of the determinate types, and see what happens in the F1's. We need to cross it and find the combining ability that can change the trait into giving heterosis with all the other traits we need. The second part is that there are now a lot of heirloom germplasm where you have trusses. Each truss has more than 50-60 flowers but all of them do not become a fruit. So how do we make the right breeding process and then combine it to put that in a determinate background. As I said, Jack Hanna talked about things that were not possible and he never took a no for an answer. I think the only thing is to not take no for an answer in the private sector becomes difficult because then you need somebody to support you for five to six years or even ten to do that job. We might need two years just to understand how effectively a new trait like this can be used or any other such trait that can increase the fruit number & hence yield per plant. Finally, it is the fruit number and average fruit weight combined which gives the heterosis for yield. Thank You All.